LAC
D'INDIFERENCE

Bonté

Respect

Exactitude

Generosité

Probité

Grand Cœur

Sincerité   Oubli

Billet doux   Legereté

Billet galant   Tiedeur

Iolis Vers   Inesgalité

esprit   Negligence

| 2 | 4 | 6 | 8 | 10 |

Lieues d'amitie

THE BACKGROUND OF THE FRENCH CLASSICS

FRANCE FROM THE REGENT TO THE ROMANTICS
by C. D'O. GOWAN M.A.

8 x 5½, 256 pp.

Illustrated

Louis XIV

THE BACKGROUND
OF THE
FRENCH CLASSICS

by

C. D'O. GOWAN M.A.

Head of Modern Language Department
Eton College

With eleven plates in half-tone
and an end-paper map

GEORGE G. HARRAP & CO. LTD
LONDON   TORONTO   WELLINGTON   SYDNEY

First published in Great Britain 1960
by George G. Harrap & Co. Ltd
182 High Holborn, London, W.C.1

Reprinted 1962

© *C. D'O. Gowan* 1960

Composed in Bembo type and printed by Elliott Bros. & Yeoman Ltd, Liverpool
Made in Great Britain

PREFACE

THIS book is intended as an introduction only. It is written in the belief that, although the masterpieces of art and literature speak for themselves, they can be more fully understood if something is known about the conditions, political, social, economic and artistic, in which they were created. It is a quick sketch, not an exhaustive study, of the men and women who produced the great works of classical French literature, and of those who first read them or listened to them, saw them in the theatre, paid for them. It is not intended for the historian, being only a distillation of the works of a dozen or more professional historians and critics, and containing no fruits of original research: it is intended for anyone interested in the literature of the *Grand Siècle*, and particularly for students of French, who would have to work through a number of long—and, for them, often irrelevant —books in order to acquire the outline of political and social history that I have attempted to offer here.

The great works are now available in editions which, as a rule, contain admirable and scholarly introductions. But such introductions tend to show two failings. They concentrate on the artistic background, giving the student no idea of the political and social conditions of the day; and they shine so bright a spotlight on the individual author (if not, indeed, on a single one of his works) that the relationship between that author or work and the rest of the age is not easy to appreciate. As a result, there are plenty of people who know something of Molière but who could not say whether he lived before or after Voltaire; plenty who have seen Versailles but yet have no clear picture of how that magnificent white elephant came into being.

I hope, therefore, that this book may be useful to anyone who reads the masterpieces of that great age. I have tried to make it rapid and interesting reading, and although a number of chapters were bound to be spent on the political history, I have sought to preserve a balance between them and those on social history, which are more amusing, perhaps, for anyone but the student at school. With the same intention I have not always given quotations in the original French, but have used English where it seemed that the French might hold up the narrative flow.

If the attempt has been at all successful it is largely thanks to the Lower Master of Eton College, Mr Van Oss, who asked me to deliver the lectures from which this book originally sprang; to my wife and daughters, who helped me with the text and wording; and to the three generations of Eton linguists who have so far heard the lectures, and whose questions and comments have helped to modify the original version.

C. D'O. G.

Eton, 1959

CONTENTS

ILLUSTRATIONS

Our thanks are due to the following for their kind permission to reproduce the illustrations in this book:

The Mansell Collection: *Louis XIV*.

La Bibliothèque Nationale, Paris (Service photographique): *Execution of Cinq-Mars; Le Pont-Neuf; Fête de Versailles: First performance of* Alceste; *Madame de Maintenon and the Ladies of Saint-Cyr, 1686; Versailles, 1664; Louis XIV and his Family, 1698; La Carte de Tendre; The Louvre*.

His Grace the Duke of Portland: *Molière*.

The Trustees, The National Gallery, London: *Richelieu: Triple Portrait*.

Eton College Library: *Le Grand Condé*.

The British Museum: Engraving from *Les Grandes Misères de la guerre* (Callot).

INTRODUCTION

The Century that Louis XIV spoiled

A LANGUAGE and a literature spring from a country's soul: and that soul is conditioned by its history.

This is a brief picture of the history, in its most general sense, of France in the seventeenth century. It is written in order to explain the glorious literature of that splendid period; to explain it in the sense of showing what it sprang from, what were the great events which coloured it, and who were the people for whom it was written.

It is the story of the century during which France took her own individual road—a different road from that of England, Germany or Spain. There are many reasons why she would not tread the same paths as her neighbours to the east and south. But we may be surprised that she took such an utterly different line from England.

In 1560 the situation in France was similar in very many respects to that in England. In each country a queen was in power, using all her wits to try to control a most ticklish succession. Each country was torn by religious dissensions, and in each there was soon to appear a claimant to the throne of the other faith. In each country the nobility was turbulent and strong, and in each there were constitutional forms, the germ of a modern Parliament, which could be developed into a democratic system. Of course, the likeness cannot be stressed too hard. And there was this enormous difference between them, that in France the clergy had not been crushed, nor the nobility enriched and won over to Protestantism, by any dissolution of the monasteries or secularization of Church lands.

For this and other reasons, France in the next 150 years took the road of Catholicism and absolutism, leading at first to glory and then to corrupt stagnation. Now, it is an odd but observable fact that in both countries the Protestants formed the most energetic and industrious part of the population; but they were also—from the Sovereign's point of view—a democratic and dangerous element. England, whose ruler was Protestant, took the road which led within a century to revolution and regicide: the French monarchs up to 1789 may well have congratulated themselves on their greater prudence. But while the Protestant element in England was given its head, prosperity increased steadily, though the Monarchy suffered. In France the Protestant, commercially vigorous element was crushed, with the result that by the eighteenth century France's commerce languished, her colonies were lost, and the Revolution and regicide followed after all: a revolution far more damaging to both Church and Monarchy than the two English revolutions had been to ours.

The first steps towards all this were taken before the sixteenth century had closed. And so, in this review of the "glorious century" which is the background of the Classical age of French literature, the emphasis will not be so much on Louis XIV as might be expected. Louis XIV reigned for seventy-two years, so it is hard to avoid spending a good deal of time on him; and the difficulty is to avoid spending too much, since so much has been written about him. One of the latest books on the period, W. H. Lewis's *The Splendid Century*, deals only with him and his reign, and entirely omits the predecessors from whom all his ideas were taken: even the standard French work, Jacques Boulenger's *Le Grand Siècle*, only starts at 1610. But Louis did little more than carry to completion the work of Henri IV, Louis XIII and their great ministers, Sully and Richelieu: so even to understand Louis, and still more in order to understand his age and its literature, we must begin by looking carefully at his father and grand-father.

The period we shall cover consists of three great and progressive reigns, interrupted by two disastrous minorities, and ending in forty years of disastrous war. Half the work of Henri IV was undone by the regency of Marie de Medici; and a great deal of Richelieu's work seemed to be undone during the regency of Anne of Austria. Then Louis XIV took over power himself; and his personal rule was so firm, and lasted so long, that after his death what he had done could only be undone seventy years later—by a bloody revolution.

Our period is actually a century and a quarter, if we start with the accession of Henri IV in 1589 and end with Louis' death in 1715. All centuries are periods of transition: but in many ways the seventeenth century saw more changes, at least in France, than any other century until the twentieth.

At its beginning the nation-states were already forming, but there was still meaning in the two great universal ideas of the Middle Ages—the Empire and the Papacy. Both made a final bid for a return to power in the first half of the seventeenth century. Their failure was largely caused by the action of France: and it was mainly France that profited by it.

In 1600 France had sixteen or seventeen million inhabitants —reliable estimates are difficult to obtain—compared with some sixteen million in the Holy Roman Empire, eight million in Spain, perhaps five million in England and a million and a half or two million in Holland. France had a splendid central position, with good communications and ports. She had rich soil, a helpful climate and industrious peasants; and her commercial classes were already showing considerable enterprise both at home and abroad. Yet in 1600 she hardly counted in the politics of Europe (for reasons to be explained in the next chapter); and it was Spain that everyone feared or admired, Spain which dominated Europe still, in spite of the fiasco of the Armada, and it was the Hapsburg family in Madrid, Vienna and Brussels who held the strings of power.

By 1700 the Bourbons had pushed the Hapsburgs into the background, and in almost every sphere of activity France was giving the lead to Europe. Her king was looked up to as the model of royalty, her Court was the cynosure of all eyes, her army was the finest in the west (if not, indeed, in all the world), her Diplomatic Service was universally admired and copied; and the dying King of Spain had with his final act testified to the general feeling of admiration by leaving his vast possessions to the grandson of Louis XIV, believing that only France now had strength enough to keep her heterogeneous dominions together and intact.

And yet one may fairly say that this is the century that Louis spoiled. Although contemporaries could not see it, he had in fact squandered all the greatest assets which France possessed. By his extravagance and warlike policy he had grossly over-burdened not only French commerce but also the hard-worked and hard-working peasantry. By his intolerant religious policy he had driven out of France nearly half a million Huguenots, who were the backbone of her mercantile and industrial classes. By his neglect of finance he had perpetuated the most ridiculous and unproductive systems of taxation ever devised. By his policy of reducing the nobility to dependence on himself he had deprived the nation of its natural leaders, and surrounded the throne with a crowd of needy idlers and sycophants, who were allowed to do nothing useful and were forced to waste their energies on intrigues for privilege and precedence. And above all, by his shameless land-grabbing he had aroused a fear of France which joined all Europe in league against her, and involved her finally in fifteen years of disastrous war which brought her to the very brink of ruin.

When one considers the actual achievements of that century, it is sad to think how much greater they could have been.

Whereas Spain's population had actually decreased, from about eight to about five million, France's had risen to twenty million. And while Spain's army and navy had almost ceased to matter in European politics, France—which in 1600 had had a Royal army of perhaps 40,000 men—had now a well-trained army capable of fighting on three frontiers at once. At sea, whereas there was no French navy at all until 1635, France now had a navy capable of beating the British on occasion, though not the combined fleets of Britain and Holland. She had defeated the pirates of the North African Barbary coast, and was mistress of the Mediterranean; and, in spite of Louis' lack of interest in colonial affairs, her fishermen and explorers were to be found every year off the coast of Newfoundland and Nova Scotia, had pushed up the St. Lawrence to Quebec and the Great Lakes and were already opening up the Mississippi valley.

In 1600 the French Court had been the most coarse among the major states of Europe. Good Parisians had been scandalized by the drunken orgies that went on in the Louvre and Vincennes, and Henri IV, with his sixty-four amours, was a byword for profligacy, in spite of his other virtues. A hundred years later the Court was the model for Europe, and empty though the courtier's life was, he did pay a good deal of lip-service at least to the arts and sciences, which twenty years earlier had been flourishing as they had never flourished before in France.

In 1600 France had not a single dramatist to compare with the great schools of England and Spain. She had not even a major writer alive, since the deaths of Ronsard in 1585 and Montaigne in 1592. Her language had as yet no grammar and no rules of spelling. By 1700 she had a flourishing Academy and a Dictionary, a purified language and the finest literature in Europe, so dominant that even in England Shakespeare could now be criticized for not following the Classical rules, while outside the island he was regarded as a barbarian.

Manners in the cities as well as in the Court had been refined and polished. In the middle and upper classes at least, women had won a new place as the equals and complements of men, and had in return contributed to the elegance of life, given inspiration to poets and dramatists, and even begun to write themselves. Madame de La Fayette's *La Princesse de Clèves*, often considered the first truly psychological novel in the modern sense, had appeared in 1678. And such had been the upsurge of artistic creation during the century that a serious (though remarkably pointless) quarrel had raged for some years over the question whether the civilization of France was now equal to that of the ancient civilizations of Greece and Rome.

In 1600 the country had been hardly more than a loose federation of provinces, whose Governors were so important that they could often aim to make themselves independent of the central authority. The Huguenots had recently been masters of all France except Paris, and were now in undisputed possession of over a hundred cities of refuge, where they could maintain armed garrisons in fortified towns and where the King's authority was hardly acknowledged. By 1700 the Huguenots had been crushed and finally banned; the great nobles had been reduced to complete subservience to the Crown; and the centralization of the country was so complete that it was impossible to get a church tower repaired in Brittany without prior reference to Paris.

Most important of all, for good and ill, the new idea of nationality had replaced the old universal dreams. Europe had broken up into Catholic and Protestant States, and it had been made clear to the Emperor that his real power only extended to his hereditary dominions. The Empire had been shut out from expansion northwards or westwards. Spain had been driven from her footholds inside southern France in Cerdagne and Roussillon, and in the east from Franche-Comté, the Empire had yielded her Alsace and parts of Lorraine, and even

France's northern frontier had been pushed further away from Paris.

Unfortunately the new patriotism, created by the teachings and success of Richelieu and Louis XIV, was not a matter of loyalty to the country so much as loyalty to the king. The greater the king, the greater seemed his country; and conversely, the greater (that is, the larger and richer) the country, the greater was the king. So wars of conquest, undertaken with no motives of principle but simply for selfish aggrandizement, had come to be accepted as a normal activity of prosperous states.

And since Louis XIV epitomized in his person, his Court, and his policy all these developments of the century, that century has been too often called after him. But the lines that Louis followed had been sketched out for him by his grandfather, drawn more clearly by Richelieu, and handed on to Louis himself by Mazarin. The tragedy is that Louis had nothing fresh of his own to add to them, but lived on year after year, riveting on to France the irons which had in 1640 been essential to give her form, which even in 1660 were still useful to prevent her from slipping back, but which by 1700 had become fetters, preventing her from developing further as she could have done.

SUGGESTIONS FOR FURTHER READING

From 1610 on I have drawn extensively from *Le Grand Siècle* by J. Boulenger (Hachette, 1923 edition). His facts are admirable, though I do not agree with his general conclusions and, in particular, cannot admire Louis XIV as he does.

The following books are also useful:

D. OGG: *Europe in the Seventeenth Century* (A. and C. Black).

J. M. THOMPSON: *Lectures on Foreign History, 1494–1789* (Blackwell).

H. O. WAKEMAN: *The Ascendancy of France, 1598–1715* (Rivington).

W. H. LEWIS: *The Splendid Century* (Eyre and Spottiswoode).

G. F. BRADBY: *The Great Days of Versailles* (Ernest Benn).

M. BOULENGER: *Nicolas Fouquet* (Grasset).

G. MONGREDIEN: *La Vie Littéraire au dix-septième Siècle* (Taillandier).

G. MICHAUT: *La Jeunesse de Molière* (Hachette).

G. MICHAUT: *Les Débuts de Molière à Paris* (Hachette).

G. MICHAUT: *Les Luttes de Molière* (Hachette).

W. G. MOORE: *Molière* (O.U.P.).

F. MAURIAC: *La Vie de Jean Racine* (Plon).

F. FUNCK-BRENTANO: *Le Drame des Poisons* (Hachette).

J. AUBERY: *Les Grandes Victoires de la Médecine* (La Table Ronde).

L. DUSSIEUX (éd.): *Lettres Intimes d'Henri IV*.

G. S. STEVENSON (translator): *The Letters of Madame* (Chapman and Dodd).

But above all, further reading should consist of *the works of the seventeenth-century writers themselves*. The sole purpose of this book is to help the student to appreciate them fully.

CHAPTER ONE

HENRI IV

Henri de Navarre

HENRI DE NAVARRE succeeded to the throne of France in 1589, during the final period of the Religious Wars. To understand the man we have only to read his letters and his speeches, such as the speech before the Battle of Ivry:

> Vous êtes Français; je suis votre Roi; voilà l'ennemi! (*then, showing his helmet with its white plume*) Enfants, gardez bien vos rangs. Si l'étendard vous manque, voici le signe du ralliement; suivez mon panache, vous le verrez toujours sur le chemin de l'honneur et de la victoire!

He was a great leader: fortunately he was also a great statesman.

To understand the problems with which he had to grapple we must go briefly back thirty years, and glance at the course of the last three reigns, and the wars which filled them. Henri IV had been preceded by the three young sons of Henri II: François II (the husband of Mary, Queen of Scots), Charles IX, and Henri III. He had himself married their sister Marguerite de Valois, but his own claim to the throne came through his father, Antoine de Bourbon, a descendant of Robert de Clermont, fourth son of Saint Louis. The three brothers, last of the Valois kings, succeeded each other; but the power behind the throne was always their mother, Catherine de Medici. None of her sons had the strength of character to stand up either to her or to the problems of a troubled age, and the result was thirty years of almost incessant civil war.

B

The Religious Wars, 1562–93

Much of the blame for these wars has been laid on Catherine de Medici. But Henri IV himself said of her:

> Je vous le demande, que pouvait-elle faire, la pauvre femme, laissée par la mort de son mari avec cinq petits enfants, et deux familles en France— la nôtre et les Guise—qui pensaient s'emparer de la couronne? N'a-t-elle pas dû jouer des rôles étranges, tromper l'une et l'autre, pour défendre ses fils (comme elle l'a fait) qui ont successivement régné par la sage conduite de cette rusée femme? Vous me direz qu'elle a fait du mal à la France. C'est merveille qu'elle ne fît pire.

An English traveller said of her that "she had too much wit for a woman and too little honesty for a Queen." The main blot on her record is the part she played in instigating the massacre of the Huguenots on St. Bartholomew's night, 1572. Her main claim to fame is that she appears to have invented the side-saddle seat for women on horseback, putting one leg forward over the pommel of the saddle, instead of sitting literally sideways as women had always done, with their feet on a plank. She was, in fact, such an intrepid horsewoman that although she broke her leg in one riding accident and fractured her skull in another she kept on riding.

Dangers to the Crown

Rival Families

Actually, there were not two but three families at least intriguing for the Crown: the Bourbons (Henri de Navarre and his father, Antoine de Bourbon), the Guises, and the Montmorencys. The Bourbons led the Protestant faction, the Guises of Lorraine (not yet part of France) led the ultra-Catholic wing, and the Montmorency family, hereditary Constables of France, were all-powerful in the south-east.

Religious Cleavage

A second danger came from the religious cleavage. Not only were the great families using this for their own dynastic ends, but members of the rival creeds felt much more akin to their co-religionists elsewhere than to other Frenchmen of the opposite religion. It was to be sixty years before a Huguenot would feel that he was closer to a Guise than to a Dutch or English Protestant; and until the days of Mazarin Catholics never felt that there was any harm in calling Spain in to help them against other Frenchmen.

Economic and Social Unrest

Thirdly, the country was already feeling the social and economic grievances which were somehow kept in check for two more centuries, and then boiled over in the Revolution. In 1560 (as in 1787) an Assembly of Notables was called together to remedy the disorders in the realm. It recommended the summoning of the States General, which met in 1561 (as again in 1789).

The States General of 1561

At that meeting the nobles demanded liberty of worship for Protestants, suppression of the civil and feudal jurisdiction of the clergy, and nationalization of Church property. This was an opportunity to buy the support of the nobility for the Monarchy and Protestantism, as Henry VIII had done in England, but Catherine was far too strict a Catholic to consider it.

The clergy countered by demanding rigorous action against Protestantism, economy at Court, and the suppression of useless offices and sinecures. The *Tiers État* (or Commons) asked for reform of the administration, cessation of religious persecution, periodic meetings of the Estates at fixed intervals, abolition of internal customs duties, a regular audit of the public finances

and the appropriation of Church property to pay off the debts
of the State.

Hardly any of these requests were granted, either then or
later. Persecution ceased between 1598 and 1685, and for a time
under Sully and Colbert stricter accounts were kept and the
Customs dues lowered. Otherwise not one of the measures
demanded was taken until after the Revolution of 1789.

Four Periods of War

First Period, 1562–70

In the next year, 1562, the Religious Wars broke out. The
first three 'Wars' lasted till 1570, when the Treaty of St.-
Germain left the Huguenots slightly worse off than in 1562. In
the course of these years François de Guise and the Huguenot
leader Condé (the brother of Antoine de Bourbon) were both
assassinated.

The peace was to be cemented by the marriage of Henri de
Navarre to Marguerite de Valois; but Catherine and her son
Charles IX used the chance of the gathering of Huguenot
leaders in Paris for the wedding to organize the massacre of
St. Bartholomew's night, in 1572. This was considered such a
victory for Catholicism that both Charles and the Pope had
commemorative medals struck, and Rome was illuminated for
three nights in rejoicing; but it provoked protests from all
Protestant and moderate rulers, and even from Ivan the
Terrible of Russia. It has never been forgotten by French
Protestants and anti-clericals.

Second Period, 1572–80

One result of the massacre was the formation of the Calvinist
Union and the Catholic League—"La Ligue", which is referred
to so often in seventeenth-century literature. A second period
of wars now started and continued until 1580. Henri de Navarre,

who had briefly turned Catholic to save his life on St. Bartholomew's night, led the Huguenots with skill, and in 1576 won for them freedom of worship everywhere except in Paris. But the States General met soon afterwards, condemned the terms of the treaty on political grounds—because it granted the Huguenots the right to garrison eight cities of refuge and numerous castles—and by 1580 the concessions had largely been withdrawn again.

Third Period, 1584–88

After four years of peace, the death of Catherine's fourth son, the Duc d'Anjou, left Henri de Navarre heir-apparent to the throne. Guise then stirred up the Catholic League and Spain, and war broke out in 1584, the Huguenots receiving help from Holland and England.

Fourth Period, 1588–93

But in 1588 Henri III, the last survivor of Catherine's sons, quarrelled with Guise, had him murdered, and joined Navarre against the League; and in the following year he died, and Henri de Navarre succeeded as Henri IV. In spite of the Huguenot victories of Arques and Ivry, the war dragged on until 1593, though it was only the intervention of a Spanish army under Alexander Farnese that prevented Henri from capturing Paris in 1592. Finally, he decided that "Paris vaut une Messe", and turned Catholic again: and peace was made.

It was high time. The wars had created widespread chaos. Many towns had been laid in ruins. Self-constituted provincial governors were raising troops, levying taxes, administering their own justice and aspiring to make themselves altogether independent of the Crown. Crops had been devastated, merchants had lost trade, bandits were everywhere. The Englishman Dallington, after a visit to France at this time, wrote that "more than half the nobility has perished, the people is diminished, the treasure exhausted, the debts increased, good order overthrown, religion vanquished, manners debauched, justice corrupted and men divided."

Three Problems

Henri therefore had three problems to face, even when peace had been restored. He had to find some lasting religious settlement, to restrain the power of the great nobles, and to restore the prosperity of both people and king.

Henri the Man

His background and his character both fitted him for these tasks. The third son of Antoine de Bourbon and Jeanne d'Albret de Navarre, he had probably been saved from death in infancy —both his elder brothers died young—by his maternal grandfather, who sent him to be brought up by a peasant-woman in the country, and gave him an education based on mastery of Latin and of the game of tennis. He remained all his life a sturdy outdoor man, with red and curly hair, clear brown skin, and a charming expression in his eyes. Women adored him, and he had great sympathy for the countryfolk among whom he had been brought up. He is known to most Frenchmen for his sixty-four amours, and for his remark that he would like every peasant to be able to put a chicken in his pot every week in the year. He is still the most admired monarch in French history.

His father had been a Protestant like his mother, but after a time he had drifted off to Court, where he finally turned Catholic. At the age of twelve Henri was taken to Court and put under a Jesuit tutor, but at first he kept to his mother's faith. He twice turned Catholic—in 1572 to save his life and in 1593 to win Paris and pacify the realm—but he was fundamentally tolerant. He said himself that "Ceux qui suivent honnêtement leur conscience sont de ma religion, et la mienne est celle de tous les hommes braves et droits."

His first wife, Marguerite de Valois, whose marriage to him had brought all the Protestants to Paris on St. Bartholomew's night, gave him no heir; so he divorced her, and she retired into peaceful seclusion wearing a blonde peruke, "for which purpose", we are told by an English traveller, "she kept great fair-haired footmen, whose heads were shaved from time to time to supply hair for her wigs."

Henri then married Marie de Medici, of whom we shall later hear all too much. He was consistently unfaithful to her, and his way in love may be judged from this letter, written in haste and yet more exquisite than anything produced in the salons of the following century:

> Ma maîtresse, je vous écris ce mot le jour de la veillu d'une bataille. L'issue en est en la main de Dieu, qui en a déjà ordonné ce qui en doit advenir et ce qu'il connaît être expédient pour sa gloire et pour le salut de mon peuple. Si je la perds, vous ne me verrez jamais, car je ne suis pas homme qui fuie ou qui recule. Bien vous puis-je assurer que, si j'y meurs, ma pénultime pensée sera à vous, et ma dernière sera à Dieu, auquel je vous reccomande et moi aussi. Ce dernier août 1590, de la main de celui qui baise les vôtres et qui est votre serviteur.
>
> HENRI

Indeed, all his letters show the vigour and charm of the "Vert Galant." He was no calculator but a great leader of men. "C'est merveille que la diligence de votre homme, et la vôtre", runs a letter to M. de Batz. "Tant pis que n'ayez pratiqué personne du dedans à Fleurance; la meilleure place m'est trop chère du sang d'un de mes amis. Cette même nuit je vous joindrai et y seront les bons de mes braves." Or again: "Mon Faucheur, mets des ailes à ta meilleure bête; j'ai dit à Montespan de crever la sienne. Pourquoi? Tu le sauras de moi à Nérac. Hâte, cours, viens, vole; c'est l'ordre de ton maître et la prière de ton ami." And to the prudent Rosny (better known by his later title of Sully) he wrote: "Sans doute vous n'aurez manqué de vendre vos bois, et ils auront produit quelques mille pistoles. Si ce est, ne faites faute de m'en apporter tout ce que vous pourrez, car de ma vie je ne fus en pareille disconvenue, et je ne sais quand, ni d'où, si jamais, je pourrai vous les rendre; mais je vous promets force honneur et gloire: et argent n'est pas pâture pour des gentilshommes comme vous et moi."

The Religious Settlement

It was lucky that he had by his side the wise, the surly, the incorruptible Duc de Sully to do his calculating for him. But the first problem to be solved was the religious one. He had gone some way towards solving it by turning Catholic; but this had not pleased his Huguenot supporters, and in 1597 they had refused him their support in a campaign against Spain in the north, as a result of which he had lost Amiens. So he made peace with Spain, and set the Huguenots' minds at rest by the Proclamation of the Edict of Nantes in 1598.

The Preamble is worth quoting to show its spirit:

> Maintenant qu'il plaît à Dieu commencer à nous faire jouir de quelque meilleur repos, nous avons estimé ne le pouvoir mieux employer qu'à vaquer à ce qui peut concerner la gloire de Son saint Nom et service, et à pourvoir qu'Il puisse être adoré et prié par tous nos sujets; et s'il ne Lui a plu permettre que ce soit pour encore en une même forme de religion, que ce soit au moins d'une même intention et avec telle règle, qu'il n'y ait point pour cela de trouble ni de tumulte entre eux . . .

runs the opening. And later:

> Sur quoi, nous implorons et attendons de Sa divine bonté la même protection et faveur qu'Il a toujours visiblement départie à ce royaume, et qu'elle fasse la grâce à nos dits sujets de bien comprendre qu'en l'observation de cette notre Ordonnance consiste, après ce qui est leur devoir envers Dieu et envers Nous, le principal fondement de leur union,

concorde, tranquillité et repos, et du rétablissement de cet État en sa
première splendeur, opulence et force.

By the provisions of the Edict, (*a*) 2000 places of worship
which had ceased to be Catholic during the Wars were to be
restored to Catholic use; (*b*) Huguenots were guaranteed
liberty of conscience everywhere, and in certain places liberty
of worship; (*c*) they were to be equally eligible for public
appointments; (*d*) they were to be admitted to all schools,
colleges and hospitals, and allowed to print their own books;
(*e*) to guarantee them justice, special courts were set up with
equal numbers of Catholic and Huguenot judges; (*f*) they were
allowed to meet in Synods to regulate their own affairs; and
(*g*) they were allowed to garrison 100 cities of refuge for a
term of years.

The religious provisions of this were admirable: the political
concessions possibly gave the Huguenots too much power.
Certainly the Huguenots abused their privileges, as we shall
see when we come to Richelieu. But under the Edict, even as
modified by the Peace of Alais in 1629, this industrious and
enterprising section of the French community, which included
perhaps ten per cent. of the population, was allowed to play a
full part in making France strong and prosperous; and the
Revocation of the Edict in 1685 was one of the stupidest as
well as the cruellest acts of the splendid but narrow-minded
Louis XIV.

Reduction of the Nobles' Power

Henri's second problem was tackled in two ways. The
nobles were too powerful, so the whole machinery of the
State, embryonic as it still was, was used to make life difficult
for them. Sully insisted on audits of accounts, so that the
provincial governors could not make themselves too rich. He
prohibited private armies, refusing to pay for troops whose

loyalty to his master was doubtful. He set up commissions of inquiry into the privileges of great lords and public servants, and removed all those which were found to have been usurped during the late troubles. And he began the system (which Louis XIV characteristically exaggerated) of relying on men from the rising middle classes for staffing the administration, so that the nobles should not have the backing of public office as well as their territorial power.

In 1602 came the inevitable plot to break this growing pressure. It was led by Biron, one of the greatest nobles in France, and a staunch supporter of Henri in the Wars. Biron was roundly defeated and, in spite of his "thirty-two wounds sustained in Henri's cause", he was promptly executed. This spectacular defeat helped on the process begun by Sully. Even the great Duc d'Épernon had to sue for pardon, and in 1606 Henri toured the south of France, destroying a number of castles as he went and hanging ex-rebels as they were rounded up. It is unlikely that Henri, had he lived, would have had much more trouble from the nobility.

Economic Policy: Sully

In economics Henri was only mildly interested. He did forbid the lords to hunt through their peasants' crops; and he did something to encourage industry, of which Sully was suspicious, thinking it would drain the manpower from the land. Henri started the silk industry of Lyons, for example, and the glass and pottery of Paris and Nevers. But mostly he left this kind of work to Sully, and was content to watch his Treasury slowly filling up again, and to see the scars which the Religious Wars had left on the country gradually disappearing.

Sully took almost complete power into his own hands, and transformed his office of *Surintendant des Finances* into a combination of modern Prime Minister, Chancellor of the Exchequer, Minister of Works and Transport, Home Secretary and Paymaster-General all in one. Fortunately, he liked nothing better than work. He rose at 4 A.M., prepared business for the Councils till six, presided at meetings of one or other of the four Councils from seven till nine or later, dined at midday, held audience in the afternoon and usually had further Council meetings in the evening.

He tidied the system up, and insisted on previously unheard-of standards of honesty: but he made no attempt at fundamental reforms. Under him all administration was still centralized under the four Councils (*Conseil d'État, Conseil des Dépêches, Conseil des Finances* and *Conseil Privé*), and law and finance still remained different in the *pays d'état* (recent acquisitions such as Burgundy, Languedoc, Guienne, Provence, Brittany) and the *pays d'élection* (the old crown-lands like Normandy, Touraine, and the Ile-de-France).

Taxation System

We must now pause for a moment to examine the seventeenth-century French system of taxation—if such a crazy jungle can be called a system. The essentials remained the same throughout the century; but it must be remembered that what are here described are only the essentials, simplified enormously in order to make them intelligible; and that they were subject to so many exceptions, local variations and temporary expedients that a full description would require a volume in itself. Fifty years after Sully's retirement, it took the judges four years to decide whether a later *Surintendant des Finances,* Fouquet, had been guilty of misuse of public money or not— and if the line between honesty and dishonesty was so indistinct to the ablest men of the day, it will not be easy for us to perceive it three centuries later.

The Taxes

The Taille

The taxes at Henri's accession were four: the *taille*, the *gabelle*, the *aides* and the *douanes*. Of these the most lucrative was the *taille*, which was a tax on property. Here at once local variations must be mentioned. In the *pays d'état*, where the local Estates met as a provincial Parliament to vote the taxes, a protest could be made against an overheavy assessment. In the *pays d'élection* the *taille* was fixed by the *Conseil des Finances* in Paris, and no accounts were published, nor was the basis of the assessment given.

In fact the *taille* in the *pays d'élection* was fixed at whatever total the Council felt the province would stand: and the individual assessments were made according to the collector's estimate of a man's wealth. In the *pays d'état* the *taille* was the *taille réelle*, a fixed percentage of his property, so that the amount due could be more easily foreseen and budgeted for. By the end of the century Vauban reports that round Montauban, where the *taille* was *réelle*, everyone was well-fed, well-dressed and well-off; whereas round Rouen, where land ought to be worth six times as much, the peasants went in rags, meat and wine were luxuries, the houses were half-ruined and land was everywhere going out of cultivation; this being in a *pays d'élection*.

When the appropriate Council informed the Comptroller-General of the amount of *taille* needed for the year, he was at once besieged by a swarm of great lords and ladies, not begging for privileges for themselves, because in return for liability to military service the *noblesse d'épée* were exempt from the *taille*, but beseeching him to put a light assessment on the provinces from which they drew their rents and revenues, so that they, as landlords, could get more out of their tenants. The richer the province, the greater, naturally, the lords and ladies. This meant that in the end the poorer provinces, having no one important to defend their interests, got taxed most heavily.

The assessment went out to the Government representative in each province (by the middle of the century he was the *intendant*) and there the same kind of lobbying began again between the different parishes. Once again, the richer parishes would have the most influential representatives, and so the poorer parishes got taxed most heavily. This topsy-turvy method pervaded the whole taxation system. The nobles, who could best afford to pay, were exempt from taxation, and so were the more important judges and officials. In 1664 Colbert pointed out that in the department of justice and finance alone there were 46,000 people exempted from taxation, and stated that in his opinion 40,000 of these exemptions were utterly unnecessary. The wealthier officials had simply purchased sinecures in order to evade taxation. And of course, the more exemptions there were, the more had to be paid by the people who could least afford it, the peasants and small farmers.

In the parishes the *curé*, after his sermon one Sunday, would announce the arrival of the assessment, and the *conseil communal* (parish council) would meet—probably in the church—to decide the detailed assessment and appoint a collector. This office was held for a year, with no second term then or later, and was cordially detested, although the collector was allowed to keep a percentage of the tax for himself.

The assessment would be made on thoroughly human principles. In the first place, the previous year's collector would be heavily assessed, because he was inevitably out of favour with everyone and could be supposed to have made a lot of money the year before. Then the wealthiest farmer would get a light assessment, because he probably employed a score or more men, perhaps even a quarter of the village, and so must not be offended. Anyone connected with the other taxes, the *gabelle* or the *aides*, would be in a position to retaliate, and so had to be assessed lightly; but anyone who had done up his farm well, or shown too evident signs of prosperity by buying new clothes or new stock, would be taxed heavily—a constant discouragement to good farming.

The collector had a year to get the money in. Payment would be slow and difficult, a few *sous* here, a few there, many excuses and much abuse. But he had to get the money in, or be put in prison by the *sous-délégué*, the lowest permanent and paid official of the tax-collecting army. So he had to take time off from his own farm and go round badgering his neighbours, or else find himself locked up in the Seigneur's cellar, where he could not even see his land, until either he had found the money somehow, or had bribed the *sous-délégué*, or had eventually been released as hopeless. Every so often the *intendant* would have to report that so many collectors were in prison with no hope of paying that the ability to pay of the whole area was endangered: and then they would all be released—as predestined victims for their successors in the post.

As a result of all this, everyone tried to conceal any increase in wealth, and deliberate bad farming was often the result. People preferred rags to good clothes; and many left the countryside for the town, where it was easier to escape the eagle eye of the tax-assessor.

Higher up the scale, though, all those connected with the the collection of taxes expected to grow rich on it. Since no accounts were published, no one could say whether the *intendant* or *délégué* had passed on the assessment fairly or had increased it enough to allow himself a substantial rake-off. Under a strict Minister like Sully or Colbert the possibilities were reduced: under less careful supervision they were only limited by the capacity of the parishes to pay. At all levels the *donatif*—the payment from a lower official to his superior for the right to perform lucrative services—was a recognized perquisite.

The Gabelle

With the second main tax, the *gabelle*, we meet a new form of abuse. This tax on salt was farmed out to a group of financiers, who guaranteed to pay the Government a stated sum in return for what they could make out of it. Let us suppose the Government required 2,000,000 *livres* in a year from the *gabelle*. The *fermiers généraux* would undertake, say, to provide 200,000 *livres* each. They would then appoint sub-farmers, and if each had ten sub-farmers, these would be told to produce perhaps 24,000 *livres* each, *i.e.*, 240,000 for each farmer-general, who thus got a profit of 40,000 when the payment came in. The proportionate figures must have been of this order, since the farmers of the *gabelle* were able to pay Fouquet in the 1650's a *donatif* of 140,000 *livres* a year out of their profits.

And so it went on down the line, till the country was paying two or three or even four times as much in taxes as ever reached the coffers of the Government. When Sully became *surintendant*, it has been calculated that the country was paying, in all, taxes to the amount of 200,000,000 *livres*, of which only 50,000,000 reached the royal coffers; and nearly two centuries later, in 1781, it was costing 18,000,000 *livres* to collect 72,000,000 of *gabelle*, or in other words a quarter of the proceeds of the tax was spent in collecting it. (A *livre* had been the equivalent of an English pound, but had sunk to perhaps 4s. 0d. by 1660.) This was not only because of the evil system of tax-farming, but because of the amount of smuggling induced by the tax. The country was divided into regions of five different kinds, from the *pays de grande gabelle*—inland regions which produced no salt, and where the inhabitants were forced to buy exorbitant quantities of inferior salt at high prices—to the *pays des salines*, where the salt was produced, but where, in order to prevent smuggling, the inhabitants could rarely get as much salt as they really needed. Under the *gabelle*, the Government did not merely fix the price of salt—they regulated how much salt each household was supposed to consume. No wonder that they had to organize a special police force, the *maréchaussée*, to prevent smuggling. And no wonder that even the *intendants* themselves often winked at it. In 1741 a band of smugglers was about to be caught by the *maréchaussée*, but a village boy warned them by ringing the village bell. The *intendant* duly punished the village—by having the bell (which was clearly the offender!), dismounted and publicly flogged in the village street!

The Aides

The third tax, the *aides*, was farmed out like the *gabelle*. It seems to have been nearly as lucrative, but not quite, since the farmers of the *aides* only paid Fouquet a *donatif* of 120,000 *livres* a year. This tax controlled liquor at all stages, from grower to drinker, and as it was progressively raised during the century it became less and less profitable to grow vines or cider apples. Vineyards were ploughed up and apple trees burned, and only the rich could afford wine or cider. By 1707 there were only 40,000 taverns in 36,000 parishes in the kingdom; and ten years before that, it had been pointed out that in Normandy the *aides* brought in 80,000 *livres* per year, but had caused so many vineyards and orchards to go out of cultivation that the *taille* had had to be reduced by 150,000 *livres*—a remarkably inefficient piece of taxation!

Nevertheless, the *aides* remained in force, and the officials concerned continued to flourish, largely through bribery. They alone could get permits for the transport of liquor, so it was easy for them to get the monopoly of supplies for their district, and under cover to become wholesale dealers in alcohol.

The Douanes

The fourth tax, the *douanes*, was a Customs tax: but it was not only levied at the frontier, as in a modern state, but was met at the boundary of every province inside France and even, under the form of the *octroi*, at the gates of individual towns. Goods travelling from Bordeaux to Paris might have to pay some form of duty as many as forty times on the way. This was a severe handicap to the development of industry, yet even in the second half of the century Colbert, who was so eager to foster French trade, did not remove the internal barriers completely, though he did reduce them by half.

The Paulette

Under Henri IV, Sully did nothing to change the system of taxation. He tidied up the methods of collection, and added a fifth tax, the *paulette*, by which Government servants had to pay a sum every nine years for the right to keep their posts. This had the unforeseen effect of making many offices practically hereditary in certain families, since payment gave the right to transfer the office to a man's son if the father died during his term of office. The *paulette*, coupled with the system, started under Henri and continued under his successors, of relying on members of the middle class to carry out the administration, to the exclusion of the old nobility, led to the creation of a new kind of noble class, the *noblesse de robe*, inferior to the old *noblesse d'épée*, but still superior to a mere *bourgeois*. Royal servants had always had special rank; when their offices became hereditary they formed a new caste in the social system.

Otherwise Sully merely abolished a vast number of sub-contractors in the tax-collecting machinery, cancelled a number of exemptions from taxation, abolished many pensions, kept accurate accounts and insisted on a fair standard of honesty. But France, as soon as peace returned, was so naturally rich that during his fifteen years in office he was able to reduce the *taille* twice and cancel all arrears, to pay off 330 millions of the

c

public debt and store up 30 million *livres* in gold in the Bastille.

He also repaired the roads, which was a great help to trade, and began the French canal system by cutting a junction from the Seine to the Loire. Foreign trade was stimulated by commercial treaties with Turkey, England and Holland: and the founding of Quebec by Champlain in 1608 marked the beginnings of the French colonial empire.

Foreign Affairs

Bourbon-Hapsburg Rivalry

As the country grew richer and stronger, Henri began to turn his attention to foreign affairs. Early in his reign he had concluded the Peace of Vervins (1598) with Spain; but Spain was still far too close to Paris for comfort, and the stage was already set for that struggle between the Bourbons and the Hapsburgs which occupied the whole of the seventeenth century, and ended in the complete triumph of the French house.

Although consolidated at the end of the Middle Ages, France had by no means attained her modern frontiers; and on all sides (except towards the Atlantic) Spain had footholds within her gates. In the south, Spain held Cerdagne and Roussillon, the passes and the northern foothills of the Pyrenees. In the east she had Franche-Comté, between the Ile-de-France and the Jura. In the north she had the Netherlands, including Artois, Hainault and Flanders. And in addition, the other branch of the Hapsburg family, as Holy Roman Emperors, held the over-lordship of Lorraine and Alsace on the French side of the Rhine. Wherever trouble broke out in France, Spain was near at hand to send help to the trouble-makers; and Henri saw the problem clearly, and laid down the lines of policy which were carried to success by Richelieu, Mazarin and Louis XIV.

The Savoy Campaign, 1602

His first venture was in Savoy. The line of communication between Spain and the Netherlands, now that the ships of England and Holland made the passage by sea so dangerous, ran through Italy, over the Alpine passes to the Rhine and down to modern Belgium through Imperial territory. It could be threatened in either of two areas—in Italy through Savoy, which lay straddled over the eastern Alps, and on the Rhine by the Protestant Princedom of the Palatinate.

In 1602 Savoy, which always played off the two great protagonists against each other, veered to the side of Spain. Henri promptly attacked her, and forced her back into alliance with France. He aimed ultimately to conquer the Milanese, the Spanish territory in North Italy which was both part of the line of communication and a great recruiting ground for the Spanish armies, and to give this to Savoy in return for French Savoy (which France did not acquire in the end until 1860). But for the moment he contented himself with a brief campaign, which gave him control of some frontier fortresses and the Bugey, the area north of Lyons between the Rhône and Saône.

The Grand Alliance

In 1609 a threat developed farther north. The Duke of Cleve-Jülich died, and the succession to his duchies, which lay between Cologne and Holland, was disputed between two Protestant claimants (Brandenburg and Neubourg). The Emperor, on the pretext that the dispute must be settled by the Diet of the Empire, sent troops in to oust both claimants; and there was a risk that the duchies would fall into Catholic hands and so strengthen the Hapsburg line of communications.

Henri, though a Catholic monarch (and, according to Richelieu, now thoroughly disgusted with his old supporters, the Huguenots), had no hesitation about coming in on the

Protestant side. He formed the Grand Alliance of France, England, Holland, the German Protestant Union, Venice and Savoy, sent armies towards the Pyrenees and Italy in 1610, and was on the point of leaving Paris to head a third army marching on Jülich itself when a crazy Catholic priest called Ravaillac saw the King's carriage stuck in a traffic jam, leapt up its side and stabbed the King to death.

So, suddenly, there vanished from the scene the man who had sketched out the lines of policy for most of the century. Sully said that Henri had ten wishes which he often entreated God to grant him. Among them were No. 3: "To see the religion he had formerly professed established in a fixed and peaceful situation", and 8: "To bring back to its duty the Huguenot political faction headed by the Dukes of Bouillon and La Trémouille"—in other words, to grant liberty of conscience but curb the political ambitions of the Huguenots. No. 9 was: "To see de Bouillon, La Trémouille and the Duc d'Épernon reduced to implore his clemency"—in other words, to break the power of the great nobles. And Nos. 5 and 6 were: "To gain from Spain by conquest either Navarre or Flanders and Artois", and "To restore France to her ancient splendour"—in fact, to diminish the Hapsburg power, which inevitably involved alliance with the Protestants of northern Europe. Henri laid down these lines of policy: Richelieu put them into practice: Mazarin carried them to a successful conclusion. Louis XIV, alas, could only think of winning for France new splendours undreamed of before; and in pursuit of his dreams of glory abroad, he undid most of his predecessors' good work at home.

CHAPTER TWO

THE FIRST INTERREGNUM:
MARIE DE MEDICI

HENRI'S SON Louis XIII was only nine years old when his father was murdered; and five days before his death his second wife, Marie de Medici, had been made Regent because of his approaching departure for the war. This fat, idle, stubborn Italian, who to her dying day never learned to speak French properly, had never shown any political ambitions, and had previously been dropped from membership of the King's Council because she was so bored by its meetings, and so stupid about understanding the business dealt with.

Leonora Concini

She was entirely under the domination of her foster-sister, Leonora Galigaï, who had married an Italian of Marie's suite called Concini. Leonora, a nervous, superstitious woman, much influenced by astrologers and her Jewish doctor, had rooms immediately above the Queen's, and was consulted on everything. She does not seem to have been particularly self-seeking: but she dared not refuse anything to her husband, who, if she tried to avoid asking the Queen for some favour he wanted, would half throttle her, or threaten her with his dagger, until she consented in terror to do as he wished.

For a time few people realized who was to be the power behind the throne. The great nobles only thought that the moment was ripe for a restoration of their power. Great nobles in the France of those days had enormous households, composed of relatives, gentlemen in attendance, servants, and pensioners.

The more they wished to create an impression, the more of these hangers-on they maintained, and the more eagerly they welcomed throngs of carriages at their door, and the noise and bustle of a crowd of courtiers. They liked to leave their houses accompanied by dozens of outriders, and minor battles for precedence occurred in the narrow streets of Paris when two of these noisy processions had to pass each other.

The greatest of them all, the Princes of the Blood, Dukes like de Bouillon and de Nevers, who also had estates outside France and alliances with foreign princes, provincial governors like Montmorency or d'Épernon or Lesdiguières, formed a class apart, above the ordinary nobles. For the moment they held their hand. D'Épernon (Colonel-Inspector of the Infantry) at once brought out his troops and proclaimed the effective regency of Marie. The King's cousin Condé, however, at once began talking of forming a Council of Nobles to restrain the Regent's power. But Marie continued to govern through the "three old men"—"les barbons", Sillery, Jeannin and Villeroy. Sully, whose surliness and honesty had contributed about equally to make him unpopular, prudently retired to his estates and lived there for another thirty years.

Peace with Spain

Marie continued the war in Germany for a few months, until the Imperial troops had been turned out of Jülich; she then completely reversed Henri's policy, made peace with Spain and arranged an alliance with her, cemented by a double marriage— Louis XIII to Anne of Austria, daughter of the King of Spain, and his sister to the Spanish king himself.

The Huguenots were incensed at this and at the retirement of the Protestant Sully, and threatened to rise; so Marie bribed their leader Bouillon, and he persuaded them to remain quiet. This inaugurated the policy followed on occasion, and in different forms, throughout the century, of keeping the nobles quiet through bribery of one kind or another.

Treaty of Sainte-Menehould

In 1614 it was Condé's turn again. He formed an alliance with Henri's bastard son Vendôme, with Bouillon, Mayenne and Longueville, raised an army and issued a proclamation complaining that the country was being misgoverned. They were supported by their own dependants and by the Huguenots; but all the complaints were dropped as soon as Marie de Medici, by the Treaty of Sainte-Menehould, had promised Condé 450,000 *livres*, Mayenne 300,000, Longueville 10,000, and so on. One can imagine the rage of Sully at seeing his precious hoard of treasure being handed out in this way.

The last States General but one

Marie had also had to promise to summon the States General, and in 1614 they met, for the last time before 1789. There were 140 representatives of the clergy, 132 of the nobility, and 192 of the *Tiers État*. This Third Estate had been 'packed' as carefully as the Government could manage it, and consisted of three merchants, fifteen mayors of provincial cities, a few lawyers and 156 justices or financial officials from the provinces—with no landed gentry at all. It was quite unrepresentative of the people, and totally careless of their interests. The Government did not intend to let in any dependants of the nobility, and as for the peasants, they were regarded as a lower order of beings altogether.

The nobles promptly demanded the abolition of the *paulette*. This tax, which brought in about 1,600,000 *livres* a year, was having the effect, as we have seen, of making many offices permanent and hereditary, and so creating a rival class to the nobles in the administration of the country.

The *Tiers État* promptly riposted with an attack on the pensions paid to the nobles by the Court. "They are asking Your Majesty to cut out this tax which brings you in a million and a half or more, but they do not ask you to suppress the pensions which cost you five and a half millions."

The Clergy tried to make peace, and sent negotiators to the other two Chambers, among them the rising young Bishop of Luçon, Armand du Plessis de Richelieu. In the end, the abolition of the *paulette* was put on the *cahiers* (the official record of the reforms proposed), but it was never enforced.

Next the *Tiers État* turned on the Clergy with a resolution stating that "as the King receives his power from God alone, no other power on earth has the right to say that he should be killed or deposed." This was Gallicanism (the ancient French tradition that there were limits to the Papal power in France), and an attack both on the ultra-montane clergy who held that the Pope had power to depose kings, and on the Jesuits, some of whom had recently taught that in certain circumstances regicide might be justified.

After the quarrel over this had lasted a month or two, the Government announced that "the resolution need not be inscribed on the *cahiers*, since the King accepted it as presented." They then closed "for cleaning" the room where the Third Estate met, and the Estates dispersed. (In 1789, when the Third Estate grew rebellious, exactly the same expedient was tried—the Bourbons had long memories. But that time the result was different: the *Tiers État* merely moved to a near-by Real Tennis court and there took the famous 'Oath of the Tennis Court', vowing never to disperse until they had given France a Constitution.)

Paix de Loudun, 1616

Condé, however, seized the chance to make trouble again,

raised an army and published a manifesto setting out the main complaints against the Court. He was pacified by the Paix de Loudun (1616), which gave him and his followers six million *livres* of bribes—four times as much as Sainte-Menehould had cost.

And now Concini showed his hand. Since Henri's death this Italian courtier had been made a Marshal of France and Marquis d'Ancre, as well as receiving other titles and having a finger in every lucrative business affair that he could get wind of. His fortune was now immense, and he felt strong enough to take over political power. He first got the "trois barbons" turned out of the Council, and set up a new Ministry which included Richelieu, who had become the Queen's chaplain. Growing bolder still, and believing that Condé's arrogance had alienated most of his supporters (the English Ambassador of the day used to raise his glass to Condé with a significant look when he toasted "The King of France"), Concini had the Prince arrested and imprisoned in the Bastille.

Louis XIII asserts himself

He had calculated correctly, and no one moved a finger to help Condé. But Concini now made a miscalculation which was to cost him his life: he completely failed to reckon with the young King. Louis XIII had had the usual neglected royal boyhood, and was now rising seventeen, a quiet and outwardly docile young man who spent his time hunting and hawking, digging in the Tuileries gardens, cooking in the royal kitchens, or playing at soldiers. Concini apparently regarded him as negligible, almost simple-minded, and treated him with open contempt, unchecked by the Queen Mother.

The Assassination of Maréchal d'Ancre, 1617

But Louis had made a friend of his chief falconer, a poor Gascon nobleman called de Luynes. He and a few friends used to meet in his rooms with the King, and it became clear to them how bitterly Louis resented the arrogance of the Maréchal d'Ancre. De Luynes was not courageous enough to attempt a *coup d'état* himself, but one of his friends, the Marquis de Vitry, a captain in the Royal Guards, announced that he was ready to arrest the Maréchal if the King gave him orders to do so. Then he asked, "Mais Sire, s'il se défend, qu'entend Votre Majesté que je fasse?" After a moment of silence de Luynes spoke for the King: "Le Roi entend qu'on le tue." De Vitry said he would obey; and on April 24, 1617, he arrested Concini as he was walking in the middle of a crowd of courtiers.

The Maréchal at once cried "A moi!", and put his hand on his sword. Vitry shot him dead on the spot. Realizing, with the speed of experienced courtiers, whose hand must be behind the deed, the nobles crowded off to find Louis, and pay their respects to the monarch who was evidently determined to reign. They found him flushed and excited by the news; and as the courtiers thronged round him he leapt on to a billiard table and made a speech about the crimes of the dead Concini.

Not content with what had been done, the new rulers sent Marie de Medici into confinement at Blois, and had Leonora Concini condemned and burnt as a witch. They then reversed Marie's pro-Spanish policy, sent help to Piedmont-Savoy, and forced Spain to sign the Peace of Pavia in 1619.

Unfortunately, de Luynes soon became almost as great a parasite on France as the Maréchal d'Ancre had been. He did not seek wealth quite so avidly; but he took Concini's lands for himself, only changing the name of the marquisate from d'Ancre to d'Albert. He made one of his brothers Duc de Chaulnes, peer and Marshal of France, another brother also a duke and peer (the dukedom did not necessarily carry a peerage with it), and he married them both to wealthy heiresses, while he himself married the daughter of the Duc de Montbazon, the intriguing beauty who after his death became Duchesse de

Chevreuse. He even became Constable and Keeper of the Seals. People began to wonder if France had merely fallen into the hands of another Concini.

The Rise of Richelieu, 1620–24

In 1619 Marie de Medici escaped romantically from Blois and took refuge at Angoulême with d'Épernon. Soon a Queen's party formed round her, led by de Soissons, Mayenne and Longueville; and Richelieu, who had retired to his see of Luçon, hurried to see her, and soon regained all his influence. Louis, however, marched against the malcontents and easily dispersed them.

War with the Huguenots

In 1620 Louis insisted that the Catholic places of worship in Béarn, which, according to the Edict of Nantes, should have been restored to them by the Huguenots, but which had in fact remained in Huguenot hands, should now be given back. The Huguenots promptly revolted. Louis defeated them in several small battles, but had to abandon the siege of Montauban, ably defended by de Rohan. Louis blamed his failure on de Luynes, and was on the point of disgracing him when de Luynes died of scarlet fever in 1621.

However, Louis got on no better without him, and in 1622 he failed to capture Montpellier from the Protestants, and was forced to treat with them. Everyone now pressed Richelieu on him as a Minister; but Louis disliked him, and held out as long as he could. His mother persuaded him to obtain for her chaplain the Cardinal's hat in 1622, but it was nearly two more years before Louis felt he had to give way over the Ministry. Finally, in January 1624, Richelieu was admitted to the Council. Louis still disliked him, and may even have done so till the day of his death; but he conquered his dislike—and from that moment on the interregnum was over.

CHAPTER THREE

THE YOUNG MAN OF 1620

SOCIETY IN France in the seventeenth century was strictly hierarchic. At the top was the King. Then came the Princes of the Blood, the highest Church dignitaries, and nobles allied to foreign reigning princes. After them, "les Grands"—the Montmorencys and d'Épernons—then the peers of France, then the other dukes and the crowd of *marquis, comtes* and *vicomtes,* who were of more or less equal rank (a title usually went with the land, and could be bought with it provided that the buyer was of noble birth).

Below came the great officers of the law and the administration; then the lesser officials and the rich merchants, and so on down the scale, to the millions who supported the whole structure by their work but whom nobody considered—the people. Ninety per cent. of them still lived and worked on the land. Between the lower classes there was give and take, rise and fall: the son of a footman could become a vastly wealthy farmer-general of the taxes, and the son of a rich merchant a strolling actor. But once noble you were always noble, and your sons and daughters were noble; and if noble, you could not enter trade in order to make money, nor even enter the professions. There was no primogeniture; estates were parcelled out and divided among the sons to provide land and a title for each. The system (by then well established in England) whereby the eldest son looked after the family property while his younger brothers entered the Law or the City to seek their fortunes, had no counterpart in France.

By 1600 schools were springing up and becoming important.

During the banishment of the Jesuits between 1595 and 1603 many French boys were sent abroad to Jesuit schools, so great was their reputation by that time. It is hard to say what proportion of young men of good family attended any school for the whole course, but the Collège de La Flèche, expanded by the Jesuits after their return, grew so steadily that by the end of the century it had 1000 pupils. They also founded the Collège de Clermont in Paris, at which Descartes was a pupil, and which grew until in 1682 it received the title of "Collegium Ludovici Magni."

The Jesuits were comparative newcomers in the field. Their main rival was the University of Paris. Here the course was two years of grammar (with the aid of Virgil's *Bucolics* and Cicero's letters) and two years of Caesar, Sallust, Ovid, and the rest of Virgil. Then came two years of rhetoric, with Horace, Juvenal, Cicero's *Treatises,* and a little Greek; and finally two years of philosophy, mainly based on Aristotle's *Commentaries.*

Only two hours on two days a week (Tuesday and Thursday) were allowed for recreation, and these were reduced to one hour in winter. Discipline was rigid in theory, spasmodic in practice, and student riots were frequent: in 1625 the Papal Legate became involved in one, being thrown from his mule and forced to flee for his life.

In the Jesuit schools the curriculum was more humane: more time was given for recreation and for such amusements as the performance of plays, and more emphasis was laid on manners and polish, less on pure learning. In the mid-century the Jansenists also ran some famous schools, where the scholarship was more thorough and worldly wisdom was frowned upon.* Their greatest legacy was the paradoxical one of having taught Racine: they who denounced playwrights as "empoisonneurs publics" had given France's greatest playwright his intimate

* For further treatment of Janesnism see page 160 *et seq.*

knowledge of the Greek classics, since they happened to have some of France's finest Greek scholars among their teachers.

They also had one of Europe's greatest scientists and mathematicians, Blaise Pascal. After he had abandoned worldly affairs to become a Jansenist "Solitaire", he defended the community against Jesuit attacks in what came to be called the *Lettres Provinciales*, the most brilliant polemic of the century and the first masterpiece of classical French prose. Unfortunately, he died (in 1662) before he had been able to give even general shape to his great work on Christianity; he left only drawers full of notes and fragments for it, but these were so profound and illuminating that they were collected and published under the title of *Les Pensées*.

Girls, of course, were likely to receive no education at all. Their future was either marriage or—if the family could not afford a dowry—the convent; and education was not considered necessary for either. The great Abbess of Port-Royal, Mère Angélique, described how her grandfather summoned her at the age of seven and asked her if she would not like to go into a convent and soon become head of it; and feeling that that was what was required of her, she meekly agreed. As for the women who did marry, Claire de Mailly-Brézé was married to the Grand Condé when she was still a child playing with dolls, and the next year, when he went away to the war, she was sent to school to learn to read and write. Even Anne of Austria was married to Louis XIII when she was thirteen, and received very little education of any kind.

The well-born young man who did not go to school would be taught to fence, to dance, a little music and perhaps some elementary mathematics. At fourteen or fifteen he would be sent into the army for a couple of years, since bravery was accounted the highest virtue in France. There he would consort with others of his own kind, with gentlemen-soldiers of the

Aramis, Porthos, Athos kind—or with foreign mercenaries and the dregs of the French nation. The soldiers wore no uniform, and obeyed orders in times of danger only. They were for ever slipping off to get drunk, to forage or to loot, and thought nothing to hanging an innkeeper or raping a farmer's wife. One young soldier of seventeen boasted of having 'strung up' a score of male and female peasants already with his own hands. The passage of troops through a province of their own country in peace-time was reckoned as a local disaster: their behaviour in war-time, after a battle or at the sacking of a town, beggars description.

After learning the trade of arms among these 'charming' people, the young man would come back to Paris for a year or so at an academy to perfect his horsemanship and his fencing. It was vital to be able to fence, since duelling was at its height in the first half of this century. Louis XIII and Richelieu officially forbade it; but after their deaths, in the ten years of Anne of Austria's regency, 940 noblemen were killed in duels.

Louis did have one member of a great house executed for duelling: François de Montmorency, Comte de Boutteville. But, in fact, he was executed for insolence rather than for duelling. At twenty-three he had already fought twenty duels. In 1624 he was condemned to death for it by the *Parlement*, but rode out of Paris proudly in broad daylight with an escort of two hundred friends and servants. After taking part in a campaign in Flanders he returned to Paris, killed one man in a duel and wounded another. He then escaped to Brussels, where he was challenged to a duel by Count Beuvron. As he had promised the Regent of the Netherlands that he would not duel on her territory, he returned to face the challenge in Paris. One of his opponent's seconds was killed, and this time Boutteville was arrested and executed, in spite of the prayers of his young wife and the entire Montmorency clan. Louis XIII commented: "La femme me fait pitié, mais je veux et je dois garder mon autorité."

A duel was usually fought between seconds as well as principals. Bussy-Rabutin tells how he was to fight de Busc, and on the evening before the encounter an unknown gentleman came to him to offer his services as a second. Bussy-Rabutin thanked him, but pointed out that as he already had four seconds, if he accepted any more the affair would become a pitched battle. The stranger answered that he quite understood, but that in that case he hoped Bussy-Rabutin would not mind if he went and offered his services to de Busc! He simply wanted a fight!

Quite often the duels were anything but chivalrous. De Guise once ran a man through before he had time to unsheathe his sword. Balaguy was killed by being run through from behind by a servant of his opponent, Puymorin. Cavoye fought de Valençay, wounded him twice and asked if he had had enough. De Valençay replied: "Wait a bit: stop jumping about like a dancing-master"—and when he stood still, gave him a wound which almost proved fatal. De Valençay afterwards became a Cardinal.

So young men of rank learned to fence. They learned little else, if they had not been to school. The ignorance of many was phenomenal. The Marquis de Gesvres had a friend who was convinced that Moses was the author of the Lord's Prayer; and the Marquis himself once looked at a collection of pictures of the Crucifixion, and suddenly announced that, in spite of the difference in styles, they must all be by the same artist, because all were signed with the initials "I.N.R.I."

But, ignorant or not, a young man had to have something to live on, and many noble families were now desperately poor, partly because of the constant splitting of estates, and partly because so many had let their lands in perpetuity in the Middle Ages and could not raise the rents in spite of the tremendous drop in the value of money. What were they to do? If noble, they could not become lawyers or traders like the middle classes, nor tax-farmers, nor bankers. The first obvious choice was the Army; but it was a profession which repelled many of the best, and brought honour and profit only to a few. Descartes said of it: "I have difficulty in placing arms among the honourable professions, considering that idleness and debauchery are the chief motives inducing men to become soldiers." And Armand d'Andilly, a soldier himself, said: "I never could bring myself to exist at the expense of the peasant and the poor, as do so many of my trade."

The Army contained a series of regiments, even before Richelieu quadrupled its strength. The *Gardes* were the biggest and smartest corps, with perhaps 6000 men in the 1630's. Then there were the "Old Regiments" of Picardy, Piedmont, Navarre, Champagne, all of whose officers were known personally to the King. Then came the "Petits Vieux", which bore the name of their commander—Maugeron, Nerestang, St. Luc, etc.; and finally about a hundred small regiments, generally raised by a colonel on his own.

There was little money to be made in the Army in the lower ranks; and there was little chance of rising to the higher (and profitable) positions for any but members of the most noble families. Condé was a Prince of the Blood, Turenne was a son of de Bouillon, de Rohan belonged to one of the oldest and richest families in France, Vendôme was descended from one of Henri IV's bastards, Villeroy, Villars—they were all men of the highest rank. The only chance for a lesser man was to distinguish himself by some brilliant action. As a result, all commanders, even of small regiments, interpreted their orders in the way which seemed most likely to bring them honour and glory. Even among the marshals jealousy was rife. The marshals present with an army each commanded it in turn, and none of them would be willing to perform a manœuvre

D

which was bound to bring the enemy to battle just when he himself had had to hand over the command!

In order to show their bravery, the colonels would march into battle six yards ahead of their officers, who in turn marched in line some yards ahead of their men. One is reminded of the holocaust of young English officers in 1914, before they learned to make themselves indistinguishable from their troops at a distance. In the same way, it was not until the 1640's that the French armies learned enough about tactics and discipline to be able to defeat the seasoned veterans of Spain and Austria.

For those who preferred fewer risks in gaining a living, there were possibilities in the Church. We have already seen that duelling was no bar to clerical promotion; nor was anything else much—there were benefices in France held by soldiers, by Huguenots, by atheists, even by women. It was a curious situation. There were far more ordained priests in France than there were benefices, so that many clerks in orders took on menial jobs or even worked as labourers in order to live. Yet the Huguenot Sully was titular abbot of four Catholic abbeys, the Comtesse de Guiche was Abbot of Soissons, the atheist Lavardin became a bishop, and Richelieu gave the bishopric of Grasse to little Godeau because he was so pleased with one of Godeau's poems. We shall hear more of Godeau: as a matter of fact he took his duties very seriously and was for the times a model bishop.

Priests came from all classes, but if they were younger sons of noble families they tended to live in Paris and pay some other cleric a pittance to perform their duties for them, which is why, by the end of the century, any well-educated young man in the capital was likely to be called "Monsieur l'Abbé." Religious feeling was not necessary in a priest, even at Court or in Richelieu's entourage. In fact, in Henri IV's Court it was for a time fashionable for all courtiers to be atheists; and two of

Richelieu's gentlemen-in-waiting once drew their swords and charged a crucifix, shouting "A l'ennemi!"

Yet there were many devoted and saintly priests, and it was the period of St. François de Sales and of St. Vincent de Paul, who did so much work for the prisoners and the poor. And in 1622 a gentleman called Ventadour founded the *Compagnie du Saint Sacrement*, a secret religious society of laymen, which not only worked to improve the lot of men condemned to the galleys, to help the sick and prisoners, and to aid those in want as a result of the wars, but also to improve education and the morality of the priests. Unfortunately, they became too censorious and tyrannical, and in the 1660's they were suppressed, though not before they had held up the production of *Tartuffe* for four years.

For a member of the nobility disinclined for either Church or Army, there were few possibilities left for finding a living. There was no Royal Navy as yet. A large number of privateers sailed from French ports—preying chiefly on French shipping! —but these would be fitted out and manned by the people of the maritime provinces only, largely by Bretons. It was Richelieu who started the Navy. In 1626 he bought from Montmorency the post of Admiral of France, and he soon combined with that post's powers those of Grand Master and Superintendent of Navigation.

By 1628 he had hired enough ships to send 68 fighting vessels against La Rochelle; and in 1638 he launched the first royal ship—*La Couronne*—200 feet long and carrying 88 guns, and flying a silk standard which cost 4000 *livres*. He tried to stop the piracy of the Turks and Berbers in the Mediterranean, but without much success. In 1633 there were 25,000 Christians sweating as slaves in Algiers alone, and the Bey was asking 300 francs a head for their ransom—or would exchange two Christians for fifteen Muslims!

Since the days of François I's alliance with the Sultan, France had traded profitably with Turkey. Richelieu tried to expand this trade, but French consuls and ambassadors in Turkey made such tyrannous demands on French traders that the commerce languished, and by 1660 had died out almost completely. There was also an attempt to foster trade further afield through Trading Companies: the French *Compagnie des Indes* was formed some seven years before our own East India Company. Many noblemen doubtless took a financial interest in such ventures, but none would think of putting their sons into them as a career; and as for the Navy itself when it was created, Richelieu deliberately kept the aristocracy out of that, preferring, as he said himself, "de gros mariniers vaillants" for his captains.

What, then, was left for the young noblemen? Only marriage or a position at Court. A rich marriage was the solution to many young men's problems, since it was, as Condé said, "better to start a civil war than not to maintain one's rank." (A sinister echo of this remark came in 1674 from the lips of the Marquise de Brinvilliers, who poisoned a dozen people "in order to maintain the honour of her rank.") If there was not a rich and titled bride to be had, then the daughter of a rich merchant or lawyer would be acceptable. In this way only did the blue blood of France mingle with the red blood of the commoner.

Finally, there was a post or pension, either at Court or in the house of some great nobleman. The aristocracy loved to live surrounded by dependants, and to sally forth into the street in huge unsprung coaches with as many postillions, outriders and escorting gentlemen as possible—to the great fury of the Parisian shopkeepers, whose wares in the narrow streets were forever in danger from these noisy, quarrelsome progresses. To be surrounded by a crowd was a sign of importance, so that many a young blood found a pension, or at least free board and lodging, in the house of some great relative or patron.

The trouble was that they were kept for ornament, not use, and that the same was true of the greater pensioners at the Court itself. So much has been written of Louis XIV's method of keeping an eye on the nobility by attracting them to Versailles that it is easily forgotten that he only inherited a system in force long before Versailles was built. Already we have seen how the States General of both 1561 and 1614 had complained of the burden of pensions and sinecures at Court, and how Marie de Medici bought off trouble from the greater nobles by squandering in bribes the money carefully saved up by Sully. Richelieu and his successors did not buy off trouble with such lavish recklessness: but they did at all times—and with some reason—fear trouble from the nobility, and they systematically fought it in two ways: by sweetening possible trouble-makers with pensions and titles, and by keeping all effective power out of their hands.

Noblemen would not have soiled their hands with trade, but they would almost certainly have joined in the administration of the country had they been allowed to. The *paulette* made it more difficult—it would demean them to accept offices which commoners could buy—but they could have been persuaded to swallow that. Administrative posts carried considerable social prestige, as well as offering interesting occupation. But they were not allowed to hold them. Henri IV tried to get the nobles to live on their estates, but he approved of Sully's methods of using members of the middle class to represent the King in the provinces. Richelieu carried the process further, and by reviving and expanding the old office of *intendant* (a post to which a man was never appointed in his own home province) he provided himself with a check on the provincial nobility and a system of spies which certainly kept order throughout France.

This is the century in which every side of French life was disciplined. Discipline is a fine thing, but by itself it may defeat its own ends. If young—and older—noblemen had been given more useful outlets for their energies, Richelieu might not have needed so many spies in the countryside. And quite certainly, if Louis XIV had not carried Richelieu's system to its logical extreme, the French nobility would not have wasted a hundred years in intrigue and frivolity, and France might not have needed the terrible purge of the Great Revolution.

CHAPTER FOUR

THE SALONS

EANWHILE, a revolution was taking place in manners and literature, the effect of which to a great extent survived the Revolution of 1789 just because it was not only an application of discipline, but also had a creative side. The Court of Henri IV had scandalized the good *bourgeois* of Paris by its immorality and drunkenness. The sixty-four amours of the "Vert Galant" may—at this distance—have a certain glamour, but they certainly did not imply a great respect for womanhood, nor even a tolerable standard of virtue. When the men came in from hunting or fighting to dine, their talk was only of the sports they had indulged in; they drank deep and without discretion, and a prudent or respectable woman could only withdraw from the table until the wine had done its work and the men could be helped unsteadily to bed.

In 1607 Catherine de Vivonne, Marquise de Rambouillet, born and educated in the more refined atmosphere of an Italian Court, grew tired of such boorish company and opened her salon in her house in the Rue St. Thomas du Louvre. She was a great innovator. She seems to have been one of the first people to decorate her rooms in anything except the fashionable dark red or buff—her salon was held in the famous *Chambre Bleue*. She was also one of the first to use specific rooms in the house for specific purposes: till her time beds would be put up in any room when the time came for sleeping, or would be permanent features of rooms used for living and working in.

But it was in her idea of gathering her friends round her once a week, for conversation and amusement only, that her inventive genius really showed itself: in that, and in her catholic choice of friends. For her receptions from the first included not only the rich and noble—de Guiche, Bassompierre (a Marshal of France), Mlle de Bourbon, the Duchesses de Rohan and de Chevreuse—but also poets and literary men (letters had in fact sunk so low in France that, apart from the dramatist Hardy, poets—and minor ones at that—were really the only literary men there were). The king of the salon soon came to be Voiture, the witty, the elegant, the master of the *lettre galante*. Enghien (later the Grand Condé) might say: "Si Voiture était de notre monde, on ne saurait pas le supporter"; but the great thing was that Enghien and Voiture came together in the *Chambre Bleue*, which would have been impossible before the days of Madame de Rambouillet.

Catherine de Rambouillet ("Arthénice", as Voiture christened her, creating with an anagram a fashion for the curious semi-classical names which fill the literature of the century— Célimène, Uranie, Arsinoé, and so on) had poor health, and nothing very special in the way of looks, but immense tact, charm and intelligence, and such wit that it was said she "could make you fall in love with her even without seeing her." Many years later Mlle de Scudéry wrote: "C'est la femme du monde qui savait le mieux la politesse, elle l'inspirait même à tous ceux qui la voyaient, et on peut dire que de son cabinet la politesse s'est répandue dans toute la cour et même dans tout le royaume."

Notice that it is "la politesse" that the great novelist mentions, and not "les lettres", nor "la science." The salon of Madame de Rambouillet was never a blue-stocking literary academy. The trick was done by making it a place of amusement, where people went because it was fun. The tone was essentially light-hearted and gay. But because she was a woman of taste and intelligence (she spoke French, Italian and Spanish equally well), she liked to have the poets round her as well as the lords and ladies; and because she was a tactful and attentive hostess, she succeeded in mixing the two *milieux,* to the immense profit of both.

In her *Chambre Bleue* she would receive her guests reclining on her bed, which was normal and correct for a lady of the day. Between her bed and the wall was a small space known as the *ruelle,* into which she could invite her closer friends for more intimate conversations. In the rest of the room there were a dozen to eighteen gilded chairs—*pliants* or *tabourets*—to which she could assign her lady visitors according to rank. The men would stand—they spent most of their time on their feet in the seventeenth century—or sit on a folded cloak on the floor. And in her duties as hostess she was assisted by her charming nieces and her daughter, Julie d'Angennes, who was celebrated by the *Guirlande de Julie,* which contains many (though not necessarily the best) of the literary productions of this salon.

Here there were few, but strict, rules. There was to be no gambling or games of chance; no discussion of politics or fighting; no drunkenness or swearing. Conversation was the rule, conversation about books and letters, gossip (not too scandalous), criticism and the reading of newly written works, the production of epigrams and witticisms of all kinds. Practical jokes were not barred. Voiture one evening amused the company by tying and undoing trick knots. Chaudebonne once got hold of de Guiche's clothes after he had admitted in the salon to over-indulgence in a dish of mushrooms, unpicked the seams and sewed them up a little smaller. When de Guiche appeared in them next day Chaudebonne remarked that he seemed to have swollen, and de Guiche had to admit that his clothes were tight. Chaudebonne soon persuaded him that this was the effect of the mushrooms, and de Guiche in terror was just rushing off to go through the seventeenth-century routine of bleeding and purges when Chaudebonne offered him an infallible remedy: "Take a pair of scissors and let out the seams!"

The Marquise herself teased Voiture by having his latest sonnet, which he had just offered to her, quickly printed and bound into a collection of sixteenth-century poems. She then 'carelessly' left it lying open at the page bearing the poem, which Voiture intended to read to the circle at his next visit. But Voiture at once spotted the trick, rushed out on to the Pont-Neuf, came back with a man who had a performing bear, and ushered them suddenly into the salon, bear first!

In summer the salon in Paris was closed, and the friends went on a round of visits to great houses near Paris—to Chantilly, Sceaux, St. Mandé—leaving the duller literary figures behind. There the conversation and witticisms continued in a setting of *fêtes champêtres* and mild country walks, with Voiture still presiding even though Malherbe, Vaugelas and Chapelain might be missing.

They were not only interested in the arts of speaking and writing well, but also in courtly and correct behaviour. Here again they set the tone for the whole country, and a steady stream of books on etiquette began to appear. In 1606 Nervèze brought out his *Guide des Courtizans;* in 1618 came *Bienséance de la Conversation entre les Hommes."* In 1630 Foret produced *L'Honnête Homme ou l'Art de plaire à la Cour,* which went into seven editions by 1686; and there were many others of the same kind.

And, of course, they talked about love. But it was not the love-making of the Bourbon Court: it was the semi-platonic, Arcadian love-making of the pastoral romances brought into fashion by Honoré d'Urfé. D'Urfé's book *Astrée,* which appeared in five volumes between 1607 and 1627, had the biggest sales of any book published in France for forty years, and the interaction between it and the salons brought about a revolution in the position of women. In the book the shepherd

Céladon is so upset by the unjust jealousy of the shepherdess Astrée that he throws himself into the river Lignon, only to be rescued by the nymphs of Issoire, who bring him back disguised as a shepherdess to be near Astrée. He will not take off this disguise until she utters the wish to see him again, and the book meanders on through the story of Galatée's unhappy love affair, the loves of Diane and Silvandre, the adventures of Hylas, the siege of Marcilly and a number of other episodes, until at last the wish is uttered, the disguise removed, and Céladon and Astrée are married. The story can no longer be considered interesting, and the characters are wooden; but even to-day there is some charm in the style.

This book at once found an echo in French society—and even in Germany, where it was also widely read. Women in it were treated as semi-goddesses, creatures to be respected and wooed with infinite patience and delicacy; and this worked with the charming ladies of the Salon de Rambouillet to create a completely new attitude towards women in society. This attitude did not yet spread to the Court; but under Richelieu's régime the salon was in high favour because politics were banned in it, and the hours spent there on devising new elaborations of the Carte de Tendre (the map showing what paths to follow and which to avoid in Love) had their effect on the relationship between the sexes, immediately in Paris and later throughout the country.

For the ladies of the salons practised what they preached. Julie d'Angennes made the Duc de Montausier woo her for twelve years before she finally accepted him (it was high time, as she was then forty); and after all, the very foundation of the salon had been a gesture of protest against the view of women as men's servants and playthings, to be taken, enjoyed and cast aside as men pleased. And this was not only good for the noble lords who came under the salon's influence: it was also extremely good for the poets and writers. Till now they had led penurious lives, hardly any having even pensions to give them the time to write without cares as to how to live. The women they would meet would be the barmaids and servant-girls, shop-women and streetwalkers of the poor quarters where they lived. Now, at last, men of letters like Malherbe, Chapelain, Balzac, came under the direct influence of great ladies and women of education and refinement. The new source of inspiration must have been electrifying. It is no wonder that the great age of French literature began within thirty years of the opening of the Salon de Rambouillet.

Voiture died in 1648, and when the Fronde broke out Madame de Rambouillet retired to her country estate. But there were other salons by now. In the 1620's Mme des Loges ran a salon presided over by Jean-Louis Guez de Balzac, though, as he spent most of his life in the country, his influence was felt mainly through his admirable letters, which he penned, re-wrote and polished till he felt they could not be further improved. Balzac's influence on the literature of the day was great and valuable, for although he produced little himself, he insisted on standards of care and precision among his disciples. As Voiture had christened Mme de Rambouillet Arthénice, Balzac christened Mme des Loges Uranie. She presided over a somewhat less formal salon than that of the Rue St. Thomas du Louvre, and used to go on writing letters in her guests' presence —the art of letter-writing was highly considered in her circle, evidently; and indeed, throughout this period letters took the place now occupied by the press, in circulating news and gossip, as we can see both from the contents and the popularity of the letters of Mme de Sévigné. But "Uranie's" was above all a Huguenot *milieu*, and furthermore, she was a pensioner of the King's brother, the great trouble-maker Gaston d'Orléans, so Richelieu disliked her gatherings. In 1629 she felt things were too dangerous in Paris, and left for the country.

The Vicomtesse d'Auchy also rivalled Mme de Rambouillet

for a time, in spite of her husband's dislike of Paris life, which forced her to close her salon several times. In her salon, however, the evenings were passed in boring literary harangues, because the hostess had little taste. A wag from a rival salon marched in and announced that he had been asked to talk to them about the fifty-two different ways of spitting—which he proceeded to do, with illustrations!

The exaggerations of the other salons showed up the merits of the *Chambre Bleue* in high relief. Malherbe, for instance, in his old age wrote a poem to a young lady whom he called Calliste. The first verse ran:

> Il n'est rien de si beau comme Calliste est belle,
> C'est une œuvre où Nature a fait tous ses efforts.
> Et notre âge est ingrat qui voit tant de trésors
> S'il n'élève à sa gloire une marque éternelle.

But Berthelot, of a rival salon, promptly circulated a parody which began:

> De toutes les laideurs Francine est la plus laide,
> C'est une œuvre où Nature a fait tous ses efforts.
> Et tant de saletés habitent sur son corps
> Que d'un retrait rempli de parfums il excède.

—showing the gross lack of taste which still coarsened the manners of the period. Malherbe had Berthelot beaten in the street for this: Berthelot merely replied with some even more scurrilous verses.

There were many salons, of unequal value. In particular there was that of Mme du Plessis-Bellière, the close friend of Fouquet, famous for its collection of twenty-eight poems on the death of her parrot, the first of them by Fouquet himself. Few birds can have had such an epitaph! Mme du Plessis-Bellière must have received La Fontaine in her salon, as he became a pensioner of Fouquet's, promising him a poem, epigram or other *divertissement* every quarter, in return for his pension. This it was a truly *précieux* salon, in which madrigals, epigrams and impromptu verses were all the rage. It was in salons like this that 'low' words like 'dog' and 'chair' were banned, and replaced by "l'ami fidèle de l'homme" and "les commodités de la conversation."

By the 1650's every other great lady in Paris had her 'day' and the fashion of the salon had spread out to the provinces. In 1659 Molière's *Précieuses Ridicules* showed the lengths to which it had gone among the less intelligent. But in those fifty years the salons had done a great work of purification both in the literary and in the social field. They had given men other things to think about besides hunting, gambling, drinking and money-making; they had given writers an insight into a world previously closed to them; and they had given women a new status in society. The laughs at Molière's first masterpiece were aimed at the later exaggerations, not at the work which had been done; and the collaboration between ladies of taste and fashion and literary men had been so obviously fruitful that the salon had become a permanent feature of French life.

CHAPTER FIVE

RICHELIEU

Character of Louis XIII

CARDINAL RICHELIEU entered Louis XIII's Council in 1624; but he was not yet head of it, and before he reaches that eminence it is only fair to take a look at the master whose Minister he was. Louis XIII has received less than justice at the hands of historians—a recent one describes him as "cold-blooded, shifty and suspicious", without mentioning a single one of his virtues. Many have simply regarded him as the Cardinal's puppet. But this must be very far from the truth. The man who had ordered the death of Concini would have been quite capable of sending Richelieu the same way if it had been deemed necessary; and there were at all times plenty of disgruntled noblemen, Court beauties, and even devout Catholics, who were for one reason or another only too eager to urge that Richelieu be dismissed, and if possible executed.

Louis himself disliked Richelieu personally—everyone did, it seems. As late as 1641 he used to allow his favourite, Cinq-Mars, to make rude remarks about the Cardinal without rebuke. Yet he kept Richelieu in power for eighteen years in spite of his dislike, simply because he realized that France's interests were best served by this unpopular Minister. Even if (like Richelieu) we assume that the King's interests were identical with those of France itself, and therefore look on Louis' action as dictated by self-interest, it nevertheless shows considerable restraint and strength of mind on his part over a long period. Louis must have been a man of great force of character.

He was a fanatical hunter and detested reading. He liked doing and making things: carpentry, metalwork, printing, cooking, growing peas in the royal gardens which he then sold in the Paris markets. All this makes his devotion to duty the more remarkable. It is true that Richelieu was careful to keep his King informed about all major points of policy; but ambassadors and others who had to see the King on business were always impressed by his grasp of the point at issue, and it was often clear that he had taken the trouble to find out even more about it than the Cardinal had told him.

The moderation Louis showed towards his enemies (especially towards the Huguenots) had the mark of magnanimity about it. He was also courageous in the field, and far less self-indulgent than either his father or his son; for instance, though on bad terms with his proud, bigoted Spanish wife, he had no mistresses. He never neglected his duty, in spite of his love of hunting and hobbies; and yet he suffered all his life not only from a chronic gastric disorder, but also from the ministrations of his physician. The doctors of the day were literally no better than those of Molière's *Malade Imaginaire*. Guy Patin, Doyen of the Paris Faculty of Medicine, describes an argument between Richelieu's doctors:

> Hier à deux heures, dans le bois de Vincennes, quatre des médecins du Cardinal alterquaient ensemble et ne s'accordaient pas de l'espèce de maladie dont il mourut. Brayer dit que la rate est gâtée; Guenaud dit que c'est le foie; Vallot dit que c'est le poumon et qu'il y a de l'eau dans la poitrine; des Fougerais dit que c'est un abcès au mésentère . . .

And Patin himself spent his life fighting against the theory of the circulation of the blood. Louis' doctor prescribed for him 47 bleedings, 212 purges and 215 enemas in a single year. It is amazing that he survived so long.

Married at fourteen to the Infanta Anne of Austria, Louis' life with her was thoroughly unsatisfactory. Yet his friendships with other women, such as Mlle de Hautefort and Mlle de La

Fayette, were almost certainly platonic, and he hated references
to the love affairs of his father, Henri IV, whose memory he
revered. Mlle de La Fayette was a deeply religious woman who
retired early from Court life to a convent. Louis used to visit her
there from time to time, and it was after one of these visits, in
December 1637, that he was caught in a heavy snowstorm and
forced to stay the night in Paris, instead of going back to the
Court at Fontainebleau. In those days, when the Court moved
from one Palace to another (which it did every two or three
months) the furniture moved with it: there was not enough to
keep the Louvre, Vincennes, Fontainebleau, and others besides,
all furnished at the same time. When he decided he must stay
at the Louvre, therefore, Louis found that the only furnished
rooms were those of the wife whom he had married twenty-
four years before, and who, as he believed, had plotted against
his life. Anne, however, had always protested her innocence,
and she was no doubt ready to catch at a chance of reconcilia-
tion. The result was a brief period of better relations, and the
birth, at last, of an heir to the Crown in September 1638.

Richelieu's Aims

Such was the man whom Richelieu set out to make into the
master of Europe—for that was his objective from the start.
He wrote later:

> Lorsque Votre Majesté se résolut de me donner en même temps et l'entrée
> de ses Conseils et grande part en sa Confiance pour la direction de ses
> affaires, je puis dire avec vérité que les Huguenots partageaient l'État
> avec Elle, que les Grands se conduisaient comme s'ils n'eussent pas été ses
> sujets, et les plus puissants Gouverneurs des Provinces comme s'ils eussent
> été souverains en leurs charges. Je puis dire que chacun mesurait son
> mérite par son audace. . . . Je promis à Votre Majesté d'employer toute
> mon industrie et toute l'autorité qu'il lui plaisait me donner pour ruiner
> le parti huguenot, rabaisser l'orgueil des Grands, réduire tous ses sujets
> en leur devoir, et relever son nom dans les nations étrangères au point où
> il devait être.

And again, after the defeat of the Huguenots:

> Maintenant que La Rochelle est prise, si Votre Majesté veut se faire le monarque le plus puissant et le Prince le plus estimé du monde . . .

There is no question that for Richelieu the "glory of France" was the glory of the King of France: the people of France were only there to serve and increase that glory, and must get along as best they could, with their own affairs taking second place to the King's interests.

Richelieu (1585–1642)

Richelieu himself was a third son, and had originally been destined for the army. But his eldest brother, the Bishop of Luçon (a small bishopric in Vendée in the gift of the du Plessis family), had decided to become a Carthusian monk; so rather than let the bishopric go out of the family, Armand abandoned his military ambitions, studied theology at the Sorbonne and became a bishop at the age of twenty-two. However, he was determined not to stay long in the country, and we have seen how he distinguished himself in the States General of 1614, when he was twenty-nine. He liked luxury and pomp, and even when in dire straits for money in his little bishopric, he still insisted on having a nobleman as his *maître d'hôtel*, saying that it made a good impression. Before he died he amassed a huge fortune of perhaps 6,000,000 *livres*; he made his Carthusian brother a Cardinal and Grand Almoner of France, and married one niece to a duke and another to a Prince of the Blood, the future Grand Condé: and he built himself a marvellous palace, now, alas, destroyed.

He was so proud that on one occasion, when he was feeling very ill (he suffered all his life from piles and carbuncles), he remained seated when the Queen came to visit him. He did not even plead illness as his excuse, but remarked that the Queen would be used to it, since in Spain Cardinals always remained seated in the presence of Royalty. Anne tartly replied that she was not in Spain any longer, and had not been for twenty-odd years! This pride, with a certain coldness of manner and an air of insincerity, made Richelieu unpopular everywhere, and particularly with women, which was a great handicap at Court. He could not even retain the influence which he won for a time over Marie de Medici, and after he had become a Minister she became his bitterest enemy.

Richelieu's immense ambition, both for himself and for his King, was backed by ruthless intelligence, intense energy, and a total lack of the milk of human kindness. He was—in spite of the cold, calculating face which we see in Philippe de Champaigne's famous portrait—a tense, nervous man, easily depressed and discouraged; so one is not surprised to hear that he suffered from violent migraine headaches—"J'ai la plus mauvaise tête du monde", he said himself.

Richelieu becomes Head of State

At the moment when Richelieu entered the King's Council, negotiations were in progress between France and England for the marriage of Charles I and Henrietta Maria. Richelieu supported the match, but insisted on getting the same terms for France that Buckingham had offered to Spain the previous year. He and La Vieuville, the head of the Council, were put in charge of the negotiations. La Vieuville tried to undermine Richelieu by secretly encouraging the British envoys not to give way in the bargaining. Richelieu, who saw from the first the need for a good spy system, found out about this and promptly complained to Louis XIII. Louis at once arrested La Vieuville; and Richelieu became head of the Government.

The Valtelline Affair

Richelieu was instantly faced with a most severe test. The Thirty Years' War had broken out five years before, and in its second year the Valtelline, the great valley leading from the Spanish Milanese to the Alpine passes, had been occupied by Spain, which considered it vital to her line of communication with her northern possessions. It was inhabited mainly by Catholics, but had come into the power of the Swiss Protestant Grisons, which was why, in 1620, Spain felt it necessary to occupy it by force.

At that time France was too occupied with the Huguenot risings to do anything about it; but in 1623 she made an alliance with Venice to re-establish the Grisons in power. Spain then proposed to put the matter into the hands of the Pope; and just before Richelieu's rise to power, the Pope had pronounced:

(a) that Spain should have the right of passage for her troops;
(b) that Catholics should have the right of worship;
(c) that the Grisons should remain sovereigns in the valley so long as they maintained complete religious toleration.

This was simply giving Spain the right to take over the valley whenever she liked, since at any time it would be perfectly easy to accuse the Grisons of attacks on the Catholic religion. Some action had to be taken. There were two possible courses: to ally France with Spain and the Papacy, in order to crush the Huguenots at home—which would mean also throwing the Protestant Grisons to the wolves; or to make peace with the Huguenots quickly, in order to attack Spain in the Valtelline with Protestant support.

Richelieu in the most masterly way combined both policies. He threatened each in turn, with the result that after a year of operations he induced Spain to sign the Treaty of Monçon (1626), which gave France the right to control passage through the Valtelline; and in the following month he persuaded the Huguenots to make peace, for fear that he would bring Spain in to help crush them. Thus in his first eighteen months in office he had dealt a blow at Spain, and also set himself free to deal with the Huguenots and strengthen his position at home.

The Chalais Plot, 1626

The Court, however, showed him no gratitude, and we can at once see what he meant by his words: "The nobles behaved as if they were not your subjects." Richelieu was supporting the project of a marriage between the King's brother, Gaston d'Orléans, and Mlle de Montpensier, the richest heiress in Europe. For various reasons Anne of Austria, Condé, Mme de Chevreuse and others opposed the match; and a plot was formed among Gaston d'Orléans (who does not seem to have known what he wanted himself), the two Vendômes (natural brothers of Louis XIII), the Comte de Chalais and Marshal Ornano to assassinate Richelieu—and possibly to put Orléans on the throne.

Chalais, a young man of twenty-eight, told a friend what was going on; and the friend said he would himself denounce the plot if Chalais did not at once go and confess it. Chalais did so; Richelieu wrote what he had learned to the King, and offered to resign. "Quiconque vous attaquera, vous m'aurez pour second," replied Louis, and he had Ornano and the two Vendômes arrested, while Richelieu made Gaston d'Orléans sign "un acte très humble de soumission au Roi."

But Gaston was not one to stick to his word, and he and Chalais went on discussing the possibilities of a revolt. Mme de Chevreuse, who intrigued for the love of it and was so lovely that she could always find followers, urged them on. Louis and Richelieu grew seriously alarmed, and on July 9th, 1626 Chalais was arrested. Gaston, characteristically, promptly confessed everything, seeking to compromise everyone he could, as is the way of cowards. He could not be punished, so he was merely forced to marry Mlle de Montpensier as arranged. Chalais, on the contrary, was executed in August. His friends had bribed the executioner to absent himself, hoping for a last-minute pardon. But Richelieu offered a pardon to two other criminals if they would carry out the execution, and these amateurs took thirty-four blows to cut off his head.

Ornano and the elder Vendôme died in prison: the younger Vendôme was only released in 1630. Mme de Chevreuse went into exile for a time. Although Anne of Austria protested vigorously that she had had no knowledge of the plot, Louis believed to the end that she had been aware of the scheme to remove himself and put Gaston on the throne, after which Gaston was to marry her. He never entirely forgave Anne, and said on his death-bed: "En l'état où je suis je dois lui pardonner; mais je ne dois pas la croire."

Richelieu's Aims

Thus, in his first two years of office, Richelieu was confronted with the same problems which had faced Henri IV. The fourteen-year interregnum (in fact, though not in name, since Louis had been proclaimed a major in 1615) had undone Henri's seventeen years of work, and Richelieu's triple task was clear. He wrote himself:

> Now that La Rochelle is taken, if the King wants to make himself the most powerful monarch and the most esteemed prince in the world, he must consider before God, and examine carefully and secretly, with his faithful servants, what is needed in himself and for the reform of the State. As to the State, its interests fall under two heads, internal and external. As regards the first, it is necessary before all things to destroy the heretical rebellion . . . to pull down all fortresses which do not protect frontiers, or command river-crossings, or hold in check mutinous or troublesome cities. . . . Corporations which oppose the welfare of the kingdom by their pretended sovereignty (he was referring to the *Parlements*) must be humbled and disciplined. Absolute obedience to the King must be enforced upon great and small alike. . . . As regards external affairs, it must be our fixed policy to check the progress of Spain. Wherever that nation aims at increasing its power and extending its territory, our one

object must be to fortify and dig ourselves in, whilst making open doors into neighbouring States, so that we can safeguard them against Spanish oppression, whenever occasion may arise. In order to effect this, the first thing to be done is to become powerful at sea: for the sea is an open door to every State in the world. Secondly, we must think of fortifying Metz, and if possible of advancing to Strasbourg, so as to command an entry into Germany; but this will take time, and must be done with great caution, tact, and secrecy.

The tasks, in fact, were to break the political power of the Huguenots (not, as we shall see, to institute religious persecution again); to make it impossible for the nobles to stage conspiracies and revolts; and, having made the Crown strong at home, to make it feared abroad by a victory over the Hapsburgs.

The Religious Battle

The idea of religious toleration was nowhere very strong yet. In England Catholic "recusants" were still liable to fines and excluded from public office; and in central Europe the Thirty Years' War was just entering its second phase, and was still a religious struggle. Bohemia had, within the last five years, been forcibly re-converted to Catholicism; and in France feelings were running high. Only about one and a half million Frenchmen out of sixteen million were Protestants: but they were not evenly distributed over the country, and there were areas in in the south-east and south-west (*e.g.*, the old Albigensian areas) where they were in a majority.

In Catholic parts of France Huguenot funeral processions were insulted, churches were pulled down, even houses were burnt, sometimes with the inhabitants inside them; and in the Huguenot cities of refuge the same things were liable to happen to Catholics. Catholics were furious that Huguenots refused to take their hats off when the Sacrament passed in the streets: after all, the King himself, if he met the Host in procession, would always turn aside to escort it for a short distance in order to show respect. Huguenots, on the other hand, denounced the Pope as Antichrist and Roman Catholics as idolaters. Each side felt much closer to members of the same faith elsewhere—in Spain or Holland, the Empire or England—than to other Frenchmen of a different creed.

The Huguenots were politically only a loose federation of self-governing communities: but they were united through their synods. Each congregation had a consistory, each consistory sent deputies to a regional *colloque*, each *colloque* sent deputies to a provincial synod, and all the provincial synods were represented in the national synod. And, in fairness to Richelieu, it must be admitted that the Huguenots had abused the freedom given them by the Edict of Nantes. We have seen how often they rose, or threatened to rise, during the interregnum. Their leader Bouillon had been implicated in Biron's plot even under Henri IV, and had had to flee to Germany. In 1619, when his protégé the Elector Palatine became King of Bohemia for a few months, he sneered at the Court of Louis XIII under de Luynes with the words: "On fait des nobles en foule à Paris, mais ici chez moi nous faisons des rois."

Richelieu maintained that even Henri IV himself had grown exasperated with Huguenot intransigence before his death—and, remembering some of the things that Henri's Protestant contemporary Elizabeth had to say about the Puritans, Richelieu may well have been right. In any case, they had certainly hampered French operations against Spain during the Valtelline affair. So Richelieu quietly fortified the Ile de Ré, near the Huguenot stronghold of La Rochelle, and waited for a chance to attack.

The Siege of La Rochelle, 1627–28

In July 1627 Buckingham, alarmed at the peace which had just been made between France and Spain, led an expedition to La Rochelle (he took a month to sail there from Portsmouth).

Instead of landing his forces in the town to help and encourage the Huguenots, he turned aside to attack the Ile de Ré. Richelieu and Louis massed more and more men before La Rochelle itself—seventeen regiments by early November. On November 7th Schomberg slipped six of these regiments across into the Ré fortifications, and the British found themselves outnumbered. Defeated, Buckingham re-embarked his troops and sailed back to England, leaving the Rochellais to fend for themselves.

However, they bravely held out on their own, and the siege lasted a year. In six months Louis' engineer Metezeau constructed a mole across the entrance to the harbour, which frightened away two English relief expeditions. Inside the town Jean Guiton was elected Mayor to carry on the fight to the death, but in spite of desperate measures, such as driving all "useless mouths"—the old, the women and children—out of the town (so that they perished miserably between the lines, because the Royal forces would not let them through), the departure of the second British fleet broke even the survivors' courage. Some 15,000 Rochellais had perished, and when the rest surrendered, they were walking skeletons who could hardly drag themselves into the streets to see Louis' troops march in.

Peace with the Huguenots, 1629

There were no executions. The walls of the city were razed to the ground, a number of churches were restored to Catholic use, and a new Catholic bishopric was created there—a neighbour to Richelieu's own bishopric of Luçon. There was then a slight pause in the operations, while French forces moved to support the Duc de Nevers' claim to the Duchy of Mantua. But in the spring of 1629 the remaining Huguenot forces were beaten in a campaign in the Cévennes, and the religious question was settled for another fifty years by the Peace of Alais (June 1629).

Richelieu and Louis (wiser than his son) allowed the Huguenots to keep their freedom of worship, but took away all their political privileges, their cities of refuge and their right to autonomous rule. As a result the Huguenots gave no more trouble. During the rebellion of the Frondes, twenty years later, they remained quiet and loyal to the Crown; and one of the greatest of their leaders, de Rohan, took service in the King's army and became one of its foremost generals.

Intrigues of the Nobles

The power of the nobles was less easy to break. Discontent among them was a hydra-like monster, and in spite of both spies and severe reprisals, plots against the Cardinal continued to break out until the end of the reign. There were four main episodes after the Chalais affair: the Journée des Dupes in 1630, the revolt of Gaston d'Orléans and Montmorency in 1632, the intrigues of Anne of Austria and Mme de Chevreuse in 1637, and the Cinq-Mars plot in 1642.

The Journée des Dupes

In 1630 Louis fell very ill with dysentery, and thought he was dying. He was cared for by his wife and by the Queen Mother, who had now become Richelieu's bitterest enemy. When Louis felt weakest, they got him to promise to dismiss Richelieu if he recovered. When he did recover he was, of course, sorry for the rash promise, and he warned the Cardinal of what he had done. Richelieu tried desperately to win Marie de Medici over with flattery, but failed—we have already mentioned what a handicap it was to him that women found him repellent. On November 10th Marie got Louis alone in the Luxembourg Palace and demanded that he should carry out his promise. Richelieu, warned, found a back way into the room, and a fearful scene followed between the three of them.

At the end of it Marie thought that she had won her point, and went off to boast of her success, while Louis left for Versailles, the small hunting lodge that he loved. All the courtiers abandoned Richelieu and flocked to pay court to the Queen Mother and to the Keeper of the Seals, who expected to take Richelieu's place; but Richelieu followed Louis out to Versailles, and soon, to the dismay of the courtiers, word went round that he had been "very well received" there and given rooms immediately above the King's.

The plot had evidently failed, and the plotters soon felt the results. Various grandees were exiled to their estates or imprisoned; the Keeper of the Seals was exiled from France, and his brother was arrested and tried before a special court, on a charge of having pocketed his soldiers' pay and swindled the Government by charging for double rations. It is an illuminating comment on the morality of the day that he himself burst out at his trial: "Mais il n'est question que de paille et de foin dans ce procès; il n'y a de quoi fouetter un page!" Nevertheless, he was condemned and executed. And the prime mover of the whole affair, Marie herself, left for the Spanish Netherlands in the following spring, and died there eleven years later without ever having returned to France.

The Revolt of Gaston d'Orléans

On the Journée des Dupes itself Gaston d'Orléans had kept quiet; but early in the following year he insulted the Cardinal and fled to Orléans. Chased from there by Royal troops, he took refuge in Lorraine (then an independent duchy), married the Duke's sister (his first wife had died), and re-entered France with an army in 1632. He came too soon, characteristically. His chief supporter, Montmorency, governor of Languedoc and first Baron of the Realm, moved hurriedly to join him, but his preparations were not complete and his troops were ill-equipped and ill-disciplined. They were easily defeated

by Schomberg at the battle of Castelnaudary, and Montmorency was at once tried by the *Parlement* of Toulouse,
condemned and executed within two months. Gaston himself
made peace at Béziers, and promised to abandon all his former
friends and to be "particularly fond of his cousin the Cardinal
Richelieu."

Anne of Austria and Mme de Chevreuse

However, the intrigues did not stop. In 1633 the Duchesse
de Chevreuse (ex-Duchesse de Luynes), a great beauty who
adored plots of all kinds, persuaded the new Keeper of the
Seals, Châteauneuf, to betray Richelieu; but he was caught by
the Cardinal's spies and executed. Then, in 1635, Richelieu
brought France openly into the Thirty Years' War against the
family of Anne of Austria; and Mme de Chevreuse persuaded
Anne to transmit to her all she could discover about the
French plans, which she in turn promptly sent on to Anne's
brother, the Cardinal-Infant, governor of the Spanish Netherlands. It was four years before Richelieu could get any proof
of what was going on (the lady must have been a skilful plotter),
but at last he intercepted a letter, and various go-betweens then
broke down under torture. Louis was furious at this new proof
of his wife's treachery. Mme de Chevreuse, dressed up as a page,
rode across half of France and escaped to Spain. Anne had to
humble herself before the King and Cardinal, and promise never
to have any further communication with the King's enemies.

Cinq-Mars, 1642

For a time there was a little peace, but then came the Cinq-
Mars affair. Henri d'Effiat, Baron de Cinq-Mars, was a handsome and charming young man who had been chosen by
Richelieu for the job of both amusing and spying on the
ageing Louis. He found the task very irksome, as Louis was
by now fond of spending more and more time away from

Paris, hunting with only a handful of friends. Cinq-Mars kept slipping away; Richelieu kept finding out and scolding him; and finally Cinq-Mars turned on the hand that fed him. He was certainly aware of an abortive plot by the Comte de Soissons in 1641 to depose Richelieu and bring in the Spaniards. In March 1642 he joined the intrigues of Gaston d'Orléans and the irrepressible Duc de Bouillon, and signed a treaty with the Spaniards, against whom the King was fighting a campaign in Roussillon, in the eastern Pyrenees.

At first, when he had been rude about Richelieu in Louis' presence, the King had only smiled and seemed to approve; but later he grew suspicious of the young man and said that such remarks were inadmissible. Richelieu's spies now got hold of a copy of the treaty with Spain, and he showed it to Louis. Gaston d'Orléans and de Bouillon were too great to be punished; but Cinq-Mars and his friend de Thou were tried— by a special court, as was usual in dealing with powerful nobles —and executed.

It is no wonder that Richelieu used to refer to "les quatre pieds carrés du cabinet du Roi, plus difficiles à conquérir que tous les champs de bataille de l'Europe." There was always someone lurking, waiting for a chance to catch Louis' ear and pour in poison against his great Minister. But Richelieu avenged himself fully. In all there were twenty-six executions for treason during his Ministry, and half a dozen deaths in prison. His 'bag' included five dukes, four counts, a Marshal of France and a favourite of the King; and even so, the chief plotters were spared—Marie de Medici, Gaston d'Orléans, de Bouillon, Mme de Chevreuse, the Queen herself.

This background explains, though it does not really excuse, Richelieu's great weakness in dealing with the nobles. He was too suspicious of the whole aristocracy, and dealt with them solely by spying on them, bribing them with pensions and Court offices, and having them executed if he could not win them with bribes. He neither persuaded them to live on their estates (in fact, exile to their estates became a punishment) nor gave them anything useful to do. Into every province he sent *intendants* to represent the King, and these officials were men of the middle class or the new *noblesse de robe*, completely dependent on the King and easy to get rid of if there was the slightest doubt of their loyalty. Even they were normally sent into provinces where they had no connections.

The nobility made Richelieu's life a misery and his task doubly difficult. But there must have been some of them whom he could have trusted, and surely a man as great as Richelieu should have realized the danger of allowing the whole nobility, the leaders of France in name, and the possessors of all that tradition, birth and rank could give a man, to be cut off from useful employment. If he had hand-picked a few reliable noblemen, and sent them, as he sent the *intendants*, into provinces where they had no connections, surely he could gradually have built up a tradition of public service by men of rank, who would have set an example to the others. But the ifs of history are idle. He did not do so; and his belief that the nobles must be reduced to impotence, handed on to Mazarin and by him to Louis XIV, led straight to the vacuous, ridiculous life at Versailles—which in turn led straight to the Revolution.

Equally, the Cardinal failed to use or encourage any of the old democratic institutions. He discouraged meetings of the Provincial Estates, and (perhaps not surprisingly after 1615) never once summoned the States General. He used special courts of justice rather than the existing courts, in order to get what he wanted done more rapidly; and he made no attempt to tidy up the jungle of the legal and administrative system.

Richelieu's Financial Weakness

In commerce he showed no interest, and he made no

attempt to clear up the financial chaos: in fact, he made it worse by his continual demands for money for the wars. As long as the money was raised, he did not care how. He used all sorts of financial expedients, even taxing the clergy on income in 1641, and inventing the *double paulette*. Under the latter, the holder of an office bought by payment of the *paulette* was deemed only to have the right to it for six months in the year. The other six months were offered for sale—and of course the existing holders rapidly paid a second *paulette* for the second half-year, rather than see some stranger come in and take over their functions every six months.

He had no hesitation, when in financial difficulties, in holding back a quarter's pay from all officers, or a quarter's interest on the State debts, the *rentes*. This was not only dishonest, but encouraged dishonesty, since a man who never knew whether his pay would come through regularly would naturally be inclined to make everything he could out of his job in other ways. And Richelieu used shifts like these in spite of the fact that the taxes were quadrupled during his Ministry. There were two serious peasants' revolts against taxation, and almost annual minor ones. In 1639 the whole of Normandy rose under a priest called Jean Va-Nu-Pieds, partly because of a suspicion that the *gabelle* was going to be introduced into the province, which had hitherto been exempt. Richelieu did not deal any more tenderly with the peasants than with the nobles. The province was laid waste, and the Cardinal wrote: "On ne saurait faire un trop grand exemple. Outre le châtiment des particuliers, il faut raser les murailles des villes." He had an iron hand, which was felt by both great and small.

Foreign Affairs
France's Entry into the Thirty Years' War

Nor was it an age of kindness, or of pity for the poor. The

Thirty Years' War had by 1639 reached its last and most horrible phase, when whole provinces of Germany lay waste and untilled, their inhabitants—those of them who still survived —having taken to the woods to live on roots and berries and occasionally by cannibalism, or else having joined the sad hordes of camp-followers who trailed around behind the armies, picking up the crumbs that the soldiers left them. By now France was an open protagonist in the war; and in order to understand her position, and Richelieu's foreign policy, it is necessary to go back to the outbreak of the struggle in 1619.

In that year the Protestants made a supreme effort to capture control of the Empire. There were seven Electors—three Catholic archbishops, the kings of Bohemia and Saxony, and the princes of Brandenburg and the Palatinate. The last three of these were Protestants; and in 1619 the Bohemians rebelled against their elected king, Ferdinand of Styria, a Hapsburg, and invited Frederick of the Palatinate to become King of Bohemia, which would have given the Protestants four votes to three in the Electoral College, when it came to choosing a new Emperor.

The Thirty Years' War: Bohemian Phase

Frederick, alas, was brave but incompetent; and his new Czech subjects would not give him proper support in the war which immediately broke out. Within a year he had been driven out of Bohemia and even out of his own Palatinate; Bohemia was forcibly converted to Catholicism in the next two years, and half the Palatinate, with the Electoral dignity, was given to Ferdinand's supporter Maximilian of Bavaria. Ferdinand himself was elected Emperor, voting for himself as King of Bohemia.

Danish Phase

The establishment of Catholic rule in the Palatinate gave the

Hapsburgs control of the Rhine, which severely endangered
Holland (still coveted by Spain) and frightened the Protestant
princes of the north. In 1625 Christian of Denmark marched
south to help the Protestants, and incidentally to stake his
claim to much of the Baltic coast. Ferdinand recruited a huge
army under Wallenstein, an adventurer who had grown rich
on the spoils of Bohemia; and Wallenstein drove Christian
back into Denmark, invaded it, and forced the Danes to sign
the ignominious Peace of Lübeck in 1629. Thereupon Ferdinand,
now at the height of his power, issued the Edict of Restitution,
which ordered the Protestants to restore to the Catholics all
lands which had become Protestant since 1552.

But it did not suit the German princes of either faith to see
the Emperor becoming so powerful; in particular, they
maintained that he had no right to hand over the Electoral
dignity from the Palatinate to Bavaria, and they were afraid of
the growing power of Wallenstein. Ferdinand himself was
becoming doubtful of his power over this newcomer, who had
been made Duke of Mecklenburg and now called himself
"General of the Baltic."

Nor did it suit the Protestants to have to give up the
bishoprics of Bremen and Magdeburg and a large number of
other towns and territories under the Edict of Restitution.
Least of all did it suit France to see the Hapsburg power
increasing. Spain was not engaged in the war, nominally, but
she was in fact Ferdinand's paymaster, and any increase in the
Imperial power was a victory for the Spanish Hapsburgs as
well.

Swedish Phase

Richelieu did not yet feel firm enough in the saddle in France
to intervene (it was not yet twenty years since Henri IV had
been assassinated by a Catholic for "betraying the faith" by his
alliance with the German Protestants). But there was another

F

possible champion who could be brought in to revive the Protestant cause: Gustavus Adolphus of Sweden. He had been tied up in a war with Poland. Now Richelieu helped him to make peace in the eastern Baltic; and when Gustavus had landed in Stettin and forced Wallenstein to raise the siege of Stralsund (July 1630), Richelieu made a treaty with him, promising him a million *livres* a year so long as he kept the field with 36,000 men.

The Cardinal knew that the Swedes were well trained, patriotic, filled with justifiable confidence in their King's leadership, and sternly Protestant; and as such, he knew they were worth more than twice as many mercenary soldiers under generals like Wallenstein or the Bavarian general Tilly.

By the agreement Gustavus was to leave alone the territories of the German Catholic League, which Richelieu was trying, not unsuccessfully, to detach from their allegiance to Ferdinand. But after the horrible sack of Magdeburg by Tilly, when 20,000 citizens were murdered and the city burned to the ground, and after Gustavus had avenged himself with the great victory of Breitenfeld in 1631, instead of marching on Vienna as Richelieu had hoped, Gustavus turned west to the Rhineland. At one moment he even crossed the Rhine, and when Richelieu sent a letter of protest, he sent back a rude answer including the sentence: "If His Majesty of France should anger him much, he knows the way to Paris and he has hungry soldiers who will eat and drink as heartily in France as in Germany."

With the armies sweeping to and fro across Germany, that area was gradually reduced almost to a desert. The troops lived on the country, but normal farming was impossible when the locust plague of soldiers descended on it so often, and soon there was little even for the troops to eat. The less there was, the more brutal they became, torturing the peasants to make them reveal where they had hidden their last stocks of food and

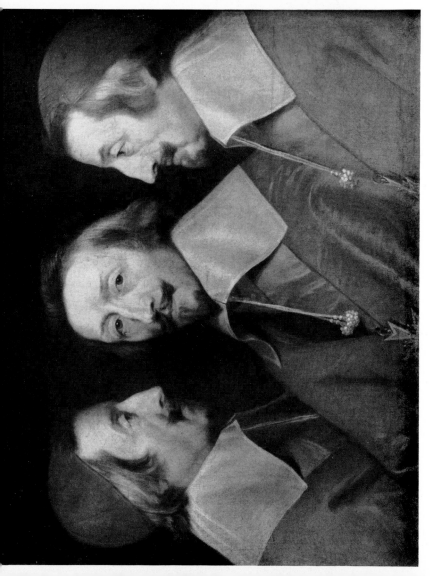

Richelieu:
Triple Portrait
Philippe de Champaigne

82

Ceux que Mars entrient de ses actes meschans
Accommodent ainsi les pauures gens des champs,

Ils les font prisonniers, ils bruslent leurs villages,
Et sur le bestail mesme exercent des rauages.

Sans que la peine des Loix nonplus que le deuoir
Ny les pleurs et les cris les puissent esmouuoir

Callot. March. exc. Cum Priuil. Regis

An engraving from "Les Grandes Misères de la Guerre"

money. And so the vicious circle went on and on, till perhaps a quarter of the population had perished, dead men were found with grass in their mouths, hundreds of villages were empty and towns had lost half their inhabitants. Inevitably, culture and learning had been brought to a standstill, a general mood of hopelessness and cynicism covered the whole area, and civilization in Germany had been set back by a century at least. Superstition reigned in place of religion. Wallenstein himself would do nothing without consulting his astrologer; and in two years in the bishopric of Würzburg 9000 "witches and wizards" were burned at the stake, while 1000 were burned in a single year in Silesia.

But none of this troubled Richelieu in his determination to break the Hapsburg power. In 1632 Gustavus, still paid by France, occupied Bavaria; but he was forced to march north again to save Nuremberg from Wallenstein (dismissed by Ferdinand in 1630, but now back in command), and in the subsequent manœuvring the armies met at Lützen. The Swedes won the battle, but Gustavus Adolphus was killed.

France enters the War

Fighting continued for three years before France came in openly; but in 1634 the Swedes were severely beaten at Nördlingen by Anne of Austria's brother, the Cardinal-Infant; and in 1635 the two main Protestant German princes withdrew from the war and made the separate Treaty of Prague. As regards Germany, its terms were almost identical with those accepted in the Treaty of Westphalia thirteen years later.

The situation of the remaining Protestants appeared desperate, and the Hapsburgs were triumphant. So in the summer of 1635 Richelieu formally declared war on Spain, and the war became openly dynastic and lost all its religious character. The French army had been built up from about 40,000 to 140,000, but it lacked discipline and experience, and for the first few years it was uniformly unsuccessful. Condé made a feeble attempt to capture Franche-Comté, as a result of which the Emperor declared war on France in 1636; and in that same year, the "année de Corbie", the Cardinal-Infant invaded France from the north and reached Compiègne and the village of Corbie, only seventy miles from Paris.

Panic seized the capital. Richelieu's guards were hissed in the streets and one of them was killed. Richelieu, stricken with a migraine, did not know what to do. But on the advice of his "Éminence Grise", the Père Joseph, he went out and toured the city in his carriage, exhorting the people to stand firm. Opinion suddenly swung in his favour; he was able to raise recruits for a new army, and after some manœuvring the Cardinal-Infant was forced to withdraw.

In the following year France moved over to the attack. In the north Artois was conquered. And in 1637 the German general Bernard of Saxe-Weimar, in French pay, conquered Alsace, and just when he was thinking of taking it for himself, conveniently died. This cut the Spanish line of communications to the Netherlands, which they had just re-opened further south by defeating de Rohan's French army in the Valtelline. Two years later their other line of communications, by sea, was cut by the Dutch fleet, which under Van Tromp destroyed a huge Spanish armada in 1639.

In 1640 Catalonia and Portugal rebelled against the King of Spain, and in the next two years France captured Cerdagne and Roussillon, pushing her frontier down to the Pyrenees. And at this moment it seems possible that the war might have come to an end, had not the death of Richelieu in 1642 and that of Louis XIII in 1643 given fresh encouragement to the Hapsburgs.

The Treaty of Westphalia

As it was, in spite of the great victory of the Duc d'Enghien (soon to become the Grand Condé) at Rocroi in 1643, and of the fact that plenipotentiaries were sent to make peace in that year, the war dragged on until 1648; and even after the German settlement in that year, France and Spain remained at war until 1659. For two years, while people were dying by thousands, the plenipotentiaries would not meet at all because they could not settle the questions of precedence—the Swedes would not yield precedence to the French and vice versa. Eventually, by conducting Swedish-Imperial negotiations in one town and Franco-Imperial negotiations in another, and Spanish-Dutch negotiations in a third, a peace was arranged—which is why the Treaty is called, not after a town, but after the district of Westphalia.

Richelieu had been in his grave for five years, but Mazarin had completed his work. The Hapsburgs were beaten, and France had fought her way over the ruins of Germany to the foremost position in Europe. Spain still remained to be dealt with. But already by the time of his death the great Cardinal had seen victory on its way, and the defeats of the Imperialists by the Swedes at Nördlingen in 1645, and by Condé again at Lens in 1647, only put the seal on Richelieu's work. He had indeed "exalted the name" of the King of France among the nations. He had also finally quieted the Huguenots. And although, as we shall see, he had not finally humbled the *Parlements* nor tamed the nobility, he had trained a successor who was to do both.

CHAPTER SIX

THE SECOND INTERREGNUM: MAZARIN AND THE FRONDES

THE MOMENT Louis XIII died, minor troubles broke out in France. The first dispute was typical of the new age. Richelieu had reduced the stature of the nobility, and it was five years before they dared play politics again on the old, grand scale; but already we can see what they were to be reduced to under Louis XIV—a crowd of hangers-on, caring for nothing but pensions and precedence. When Louis was dead, the Queen went to join her sons; but the throng of courtiers crowding round them made the room unbearable, so she asked the Duc de Beaufort (son of Henri's bastard, Vendôme) to clear some of them away. Immediately a quarrel broke out over his right to give orders, and Beaufort and Condé practically came to blows in the presence of the grief-stricken Queen.

Three days later Anne of Austria, now Regent, went formally to the *Parlement* to break Louis XIII's Will, which had subordinated her and Gaston d'Orléans to a Council of Four, of whom Mazarin was one. There the four-year-old King held a *lit de justice*, the ceremony by which emergency measures could be pushed through, and the *Parlement* could be forced to register edicts which it had previously rejected.

The Parlement

The *Parlement* was not in the least like the English Parliament, though at this time it liked to think it was, seeing the way Parliament was just defeating King Charles and governing

England. The *Parlements* were assemblies of the leading legal officials in all branches of the law which had, at the same time, the functions of a supreme Court of Appeal in every jurisdiction, and the duty of registering all the King's edicts before they became law. There were twelve *Parlements* in France, of which the *Parlement* of Paris inevitably became the chief. Since all forms of democratic check on the actions of the monarchy had been allowed to wither and die, the *Parlement* of Paris had tried to act as a constitutional brake on the King's absolute power, by refusing to register his edicts on occasion, and by discussing them at length on general, not only on legal grounds. Hence Richelieu's hatred of them.

A *lit de justice* was a convenient fiction to get over their opposition. The King would formally announce that he was so ill that he must hold a *lit de justice*. He would then proceed to the *Parlement,* where a formal bed (or pile of cushions) was ready for him. There he would state that as he was at the point of death, it was urgent that the edict in question be registered without more ado. And once he had pronounced this formula, the *Parlement* could protest no further—and the King could make a miraculously quick 'recovery'.

Louis' Will, therefore, lasted only four days; after which Anne of Austria was free to nominate whom she would to her Councils. In fact, of course, she did what Mazarin told her. At this time she was a woman of forty-two, still marvellously healthy, a good-looking, energetic ash-blonde. Louis XIV got from her his splendid constitution and his appetite: for *déjeuner* she would eat soup, cutlets, sausages and bread and milk—and do equally well at dinner and supper. She was not over-ceremonious: during the heat-wave of 1646 she and her sons and her ladies held court in the Seine, all clad in ground-length nightdresses so that the decencies were preserved. Normally easy-going, she would lose her temper on occasion (for instance, with some overbold deputation from the *Parlement*) and shout

"Taisez-vous! Taisez-vous!" in a voice that has been described as a yap like a terrier's.

Cardinal Mazarin

She was entirely virtuous, liked compliments and soon fell in love with Cardinal Mazarin. In fact, most modern historians believe that they were married. There was no reason (except policy) why they should not have been, after Louis' death, since Mazarin, though a Cardinal, was not a priest in orders. Born in July 1602, the son of a businessman in the household of Prince Colonna, this tall, athletic, blond Italian had studied under the Jesuits in Rome and then at Madrid University. In 1630 he was sent as Papal envoy to negotiate over the succession to the Duchy of Mantua, and arrived at Casale with news of the settlement just in time to prevent the fighting from breaking out again. He then caught the eye of Cardinal Richelieu, who took him into his own service and trained him, obtaining the Cardinal's hat for him in 1641.

Mazarin had all the qualities that Richelieu lacked—tact, charm, urbanity. He could flatter Anne as she liked to be flattered, and could explain things to her so that the most complicated State affairs seemed easy. He belonged to no party or clique, and was devoted to the service of France. From his diary it can be seen how he won her over. After a period of nervousness, when he clearly wonders how long he will stay at the head of affairs, he suddenly becomes confident, and soon we find entries like this: "Sa Majesté devrait s'appliquer à me gagner l'esprit de tous ceux qui la servent, et cela en faisant passer par mes mains toutes les grâces qu'ils reçoivent." This would, incidentally, help Mazarin in another way as well. He was inordinately fond of money, and left at his death a fortune beside which those of Concini and Richelieu were insignificant: and the royal patronage, passing through his hands, would leave on his palm many a fat *donatif*.

At first no one objected to Mazarin remaining in office, because no one expected Anne to keep him for more than six months. When the arrangement seemed to be lasting there came the *Cabale des Importants*, a plot to assassinate him, fomented by the Court beauties. His spies discovered it in time: Beaufort was imprisoned in Vincennes (where his father had died) and a number of nobles were exiled.

Meanwhile the Thirty Years' War continued, as has been seen, and at last peace was signed between Sweden, France and the Empire. Holland and Spain also made peace, but France and Spain remained at war. By the Treaty of Westphalia France gained Alsace (though it was left in doubt whether it remained part of the Empire or not), Pignerol in Savoy (the key to the Alpine passes), and the three bishoprics of Metz, Toul and Verdun in north-east France, which have since become France's guardian fortresses. The final signature was hastened by the outbreak of the Frondes, a series of revolts in France against the rule of Mazarin.

The Frondes

These revolts, called after the name of the childish sport of catapulting, were semi-serious revolts with no very definite purpose. They were against Mazarin, but not for anything in particular. The saying "Tout Français est frondeur" has become almost a proverb, and this tendency of Frenchmen only to combine solidly in opposition is what makes government so difficult in France, even to-day. The Frondes were more a fashion than anything else. The participants all liked striking attitudes and playing 'literary' parts: the *Parlement* liked to be told that they resembled the Roman Senate. The noble Noirmoutiers confessed that he felt as if he were "taking part in the siege of Marcilly"—the famous siege in Honoré d'Urfé's novel *Astrée*. Great ladies liked to fire cannon, and one skirmish was decided by the capture of the Bastille by Mlle de Montpensier, the "Grande Mademoiselle", daughter of Gaston d'Orléans. Many other noble ladies took their chairs to watch her direct the guns on the fortress; and noblemen rode beribboned into battle, wearing their ladies' favours as in a mediaeval tournament.

All the same, the Frondes had three consequences which force us to take them seriously. For one thing they encouraged Spain to carry on the war for ten years—and they included the last occasion on which a French nobleman called in Spain to his help against his King: patriotism had increased so much that everyone felt for the first time that this was going too far.

For another thing they reduced the peasantry, particularly in the areas near Paris, to a state of misery unequalled since the Wars of Religion. And third (and perhaps most important), they gave the young Louis XIV such a horror of Paris that he eventually moved the seat of his government out to Versailles, where he cut himself and his successors off from all real contact with their people. He never forgot how the mob had poured through the Louvre all one night, "stinking of garlic" and demanding to see their young King in bed.

The First Fronde—"du Parlement"

The first Fronde was started by the *Parlement*. During Mazarin's first five years it had spent a lot of time, and acquired some unjustified popularity, by refusing to register edicts imposing new taxation which was needed for the war. The popularity was unjustified because the edicts were always registered as soon as the members of the *Parlement* were themselves exempted from the taxation; but this point they managed to keep hidden from the Paris mob. In August 1648 Mazarin had two of the noisiest demagogues in the *Parlement* imprisoned, Blancmesnil and Broussel. The latter was very popular, and a riot ensued. Broussel was freed after the *Parlement* had promised to "discontinue its seditious meetings"; but Mazarin judged it prudent to withdraw with the Queen Mother and Louis to Rueil (some forty miles away) on September 13th.

After a month Anne of Austria signed a 24-article charter promising better government, and returned to Paris, only to leave again in January by night when Condé had been won over to her side to lead her troops. The *Parlement* and great ladies like Mme de Chevreuse and Mme de Longueville kept Paris in a ferment for a time; but the Parisians soon found it expensive to keep up the soldiers and retinues brought in by the nobles, and began to complain that "les colonels et capitaines de Paris n'avaient pas été établis pour s'exposer, eux-mêmes et les bourgeois de la dite ville, à des sorties auxquelles ils pourraient courir hasard de leur vie"!

Finally Molé, on behalf of the *Parlement*, made peace with the Court in April by the Paix de Rueil, signed by everyone except Turenne, and the Court re-entered Paris in triumph.

The Second Fronde—"des Princes"

Condé, however, went about boasting that he alone had saved the situation, and infuriated everyone by his arrogance. By January 1650 he had become insufferable, and in that month he, his brother Conti and his brother-in-law Longueville were arrested. At this news Turenne, who had taken refuge in Lorraine, marched into the country at the head of a Spanish force. Turenne, second son of de Bouillon, was a general second only to Condé in ability: but whereas Condé won his victories by flashes of brilliance and impetuous energy, Turenne was a slow, methodical worker, and indeed a slow learner of his trade. He had not yet reached the heights; and on this occasion he was easily defeated by the Royal troops at Rethel, and forced to retire.

Mazarin seemed secure. But he had made the mistake of not satisfying the demands of the coadjutor to the Archbishop of

Paris, an energetic, intriguing, able but unreliable cleric called Gondi, the future Cardinal de Retz. Gondi stirred up trouble among the Princes, and in February 1651 Mazarin, afraid for his life, left France. Condé and his relatives were released, Conti became Governor of Languedoc—and within six months Condé had again disgusted everyone and disrupted the opposition. Mazarin, however, tried to return too soon, and trouble flared up again. In January 1652 there were in the field an army under Mazarin, the Princes' army under Condé, and a royal force under Turenne who had made his peace with the Court. And all this time the Spanish war was still going on.

Condé marched to get help from Paris, but the citizens shut the gates in his face. Turenne attacked him in the Faubourg St. Antoine, outside the walls, and he was only saved by the "capture of the Bastille" by the Grande Mademoiselle, who opened the city gates and let in his troops.

However, Mazarin arranged for Gondi to receive the Cardinal's hat; the Parisians once more found the Princes and their retinues expensive and dangerous; and Louis was now declared a major, so that a revolt against the Court became treason. So when in August Mazarin tactfully withdrew from France again, peace was made, and in October Louis re-entered Paris in triumph. Mazarin followed four months later, and from then till his death his power was supreme. Condé went off to seek help from Spain, but his fellow-princes now felt that this was going too far. Mazarin, in spite of the fact that the English Royal Family were guests of the French during their exile, made an alliance with Cromwell, and in 1657 the Spaniards were beaten at the Battle of the Dunes, near Dunkirk. Spain then sued for peace.

The Peace of the Pyrenees, 1659

By the Peace of the Pyrenees which followed, Spain gave France Artois in the north, with a string of towns on the

northern frontier and a part of Lorraine; Cerdagne and
Roussillon in the south: and the Infanta Maria Theresa as a
bride for Louis XIV with a dowry of half a million crowns—
which was never paid. In return Louis undertook that his heirs
by Maria Theresa should have no claim to the Spanish throne:
but as the dowry was not paid, he was able forty years later
to put that undertaking aside.

The Character of the Young King

Between the end of the Frondes and the Peace, France had
enjoyed internal quiet. There had been hardly any reprisals
after the rebellion, and no executions. Some of the Princes
were exiled to their estates, and at the end of 1652 Gondi (now
Cardinal de Retz) was arrested and imprisoned. The way in
which this was done gave a clue to the new King's character.
The arrest had been decided on, and the Court was only
waiting for a suitable moment, when de Retz announced that
he was coming to visit the King and Queen Mother. The boy-
king—only thirteen years old—received him with perfect
friendliness and composure, and then, after a few minutes,
announced that he was going to Mass. As de Retz followed him
out of the room, the Captain of the Archers arrested him, and
he had no chance to make his escape or communicate with his
friends. Even at thirteen Louis knew how to play his royal
part and conceal his feelings if need be.

He also knew how to show them. In 1655 the *Parlement*
began again to debate the King's edicts—or rather, Mazarin's.
The King announced that he would hold a *lit de justice*, but
instead of appearing in full robes of state he appeared in
hunting clothes, whip in hand. In a voice of fury he said:
"Chacun sait quels troubles vos débats ont causés dans mon
État. On me dit que vous avez l'intention de les continuer. Je
suis venu exprès pour le défendre. Monsieur le Président, je

vous défends de tenir ces séances, et je défends à chacun de vous d'en demander à l'avenir." And he marched out, having accomplished at sixteen more than Richelieu had ever dared to do.

But for the most part he was content to dance, hunt and amuse himself, waiting for his time to come, while Mazarin governed the State. This the Cardinal did with a mixture of shrewdness and avarice, amassing meanwhile the most enormous private fortune, and marrying off his nieces, the Mancini girls, to dukes or Princes of the Blood. He did prevent Louis himself from marrying one of them, Marie Mancini, for whom Louis had conceived an "eternal passion." But even for her he found an Italian prince; and his personal fortune at his death amounted to some 300 million *livres*. It might well have been confiscated after his death: as we shall see, Louis did not approve of his financial methods. But he saved it by the bold stroke of giving it all to Louis a few days before his death. As a last gesture to his dying Minister (who was probably also his stepfather) Louis could not refuse to give it back to him, and so could not take it away again when he was dead: but he never forgot the years when the Royal Treasury was so often empty, and when his requests for money would be met with: "Sire, your Treasury is empty, but if you ask the Cardinal, no doubt he can lend you what you need."

CHAPTER SEVEN

THE ACADEMY AND THE THEATRE

IN SPITE of—or is it because of?—the vigorous part which France came to play in European politics under Richelieu and Mazarin, her literary life developed apace during this period. It was not only in the salons that books were discussed and writers could offer their works to the public. Even on the Pont-Neuf, the wide bridge that was the centre of gossip and amusement for the common people of Paris (it was there that Voiture got his bear), books and pamphlets were sold in profusion, many of them 'under the counter' for one reason or another.

In the early days of the century the popular taste had favoured books of jokes by Tabarin the clown or the comedians of the Hôtel de Bourgogne Theatre: and Maître Guillaume, Henri IV's dwarf, sold there both collections of his jokes and political satires of a crude kind. Later, as the hand of the Cardinal was felt more firmly and criticism was driven underground, the booklets sold became more and more political, until during the Frondes over 6000 anti-Mazarin pamphlets were produced in three and a half years. Some of these even preached the "social contract" theory (that kings only held power in return for governing and protecting their people, and could be turned out if they broke their contract), and argued for a republic; and they were countered by pamphlets from writers in the pay of the Cardinals, who could not stamp out their critics altogether, and dared not leave them unanswered.

But Richelieu's ideas of discipline went far beyond the political field. He would have liked to establish an official critical body which could lay down the rules on what was good literature and what was bad. He (like most of his contemporaries) quite genuinely believed that such rules could be formulated and applied, and he also coveted the reputation of a great patron of literature, even after his hopes of becoming a successful dramatist had, as we shall see, been blighted.

During the years of Richelieu's rise to power, a dozen or so writers used to meet at the house of the Huguenot Conrart to exchange ideas and gossip and to read their works to one another. The group had no political flavour, though three of its members earned their living by being the *intendants* of the households of d'Harcourt, de La Rochefoucauld and Bassompierre—all enemies of Richelieu. Others, on the contrary, were his friends: and one of these, Boisrobert, told Richelieu about the meetings, and of the group's attempts to judge their own and other people's writings.

Richelieu saw a chance to render the group politically harmless and acquire a reputation as a Maecenas. He proposed to increase its size and give it an official position. The suggested number of members was forty, and it was to include many of the hack writers in Richelieu's pay. At first the other group members were doubtful; and when in 1634, for domestic reasons, Conrart had to stop being their host, it looked as though the circle would break up. However, they continued to meet, and finally decided to accept the Cardinal's offer, which was couched in generous terms, giving them the right to choose their own title and write their own statutes. Chapelain persuaded them to state as their objects the production of a dictionary, a grammar, a book of rhetoric and one of poetics. Conrart became their *Secrétaire Perpétuel*. All seemed to be going smoothly when an unexpected difficulty arose: the *Parlement* refused to register the letters-patent creating them the Académie Française.

For a time the scheme hung fire. They could find no regular meeting place; they could only agree on the names of thirty-six members; and the old hands began loudly to regret the cosy

ECUTION DES SIEURS DE CINQ-MARS, ET DE THOU, CONDAMNEZ

R ARREST DAVOIR LA TESTE TRANCHÉE A LION DANS LA PLACE

TERREAUX, LE 12 SEPTEMBRE, COMME CRIMINELS DE LEZE MAIESTE

Le Grand Condé

intimacy of their meetings at Conrart's house. But in 1637 Richelieu, anxious to have his Academy pronounce judgment on Corneille's *Le Cid*, forced the issue with the *Parlement*. With a bad grace he accepted the very important change in their statutes which made it optional, and not obligatory, for writers to submit their works to the Academy for criticism; and in return for this concession the *Parlement* registered the letters-patent, and the Académie Française came formally into being.

We must now look at the state of the theatre, before considering the next stages of the Academy's development. When Henri IV came to the throne there was virtually no theatre in France. The great surge of dramatic expression which was then sweeping England and Spain found only the dimmest echo in Paris. The Church had got performance of the mediaeval mystery plays banned in Paris in 1548, and although they survived in the provinces, Paris could only see the farces and morality plays performed by the *Confrères de la Passion*.

In 1599 the first permanent company of actors was formed in Paris, and rented the Hôtel de Bourgogne from the *Confrères de la Passion:* and in 1600 there appeared a playwright, Alexandre Hardy, who, though not of the first rank, was at least good enough to make the theatre attractive and respectable. He was incredibly prolific, writing seven hundred-odd plays between 1600 and 1630, so it is hardly surprising that they were not very highly polished. But they were amusing, interesting, and of many kinds, from the pastoral to the tragic; and they were good enough to attract the *bons bourgeois* of Paris, and even the nobles from the salons, as well as the common people, who had demanded nothing more than blood, thunder and buffoonery.

With Hardy—and of course others, such as Tristan L'Hermite and Mairet—to write for them, the troupe of the Hôtel de Bourgogne established a tradition of fine declamation and good acting, and under Louis XIII they were allowed to take

G

the title of the Troupe Royale. A rival troupe, that of the Théâtre du Marais, provided enough competition to keep them on their toes. They performed in small theatres, which could, however, hold a surprising number of people: in the latter part of the century the Comédie Française could hold as many as 2000 on occasion. The hall was lit by candles (a good description can be found in Rostand's *Cyrano de Bergerac*), and the majority of the spectators stood in the body of the theatre. In the early part of the century they were extremely rowdy, and threw fruit or stones if they disapproved; but as manners grew more disciplined it was noted, as an instance of increasing refinement, that they stopped throwing things and merely whistled.

The ladies sat in boxes round the hall, and the nobility either sat with them or on the stage itself, which did not help the dramatic illusion (even in the eighteenth century the ghost in one of Voltaire's plays had to elbow its way on to the stage, preceded by cries of "Place à l'ombre"!). The minimum of scenery was used: at first only a *décor simultané*, in which the single stage-set would include a few token trees (the forest), a fragment of wall (the castle), and a few chairs (the hall). Later it became more elaborate; but it should be remembered that the 'unity of place' was a great convenience for the playwrights of the age because of the difficulty of scene-changing, and that the "vestibule ou anti-chambre, lieu banal où nos tragédies ont la complaisance de venir se dérouler", of which Hugo complained two centuries later, was not nearly so improbable in an age when, as we have seen, rooms were not set apart for such fixed and immutable purposes as they have been since. Even in a commodious house, the sitting-rooms would be used to sleep in and the bedrooms for business. So the audiences in the seventeenth-century theatre would not find it so strange as Hugo did to see so many different actors appearing and declaiming their speeches against a single background.

By 1636, then, there were in Paris, ready and awaiting

the use of a master, trained professional actors, two permanent theatres, and a theatre-going public. The only curious thing is the time it took for the master to reveal himself fully. In 1629 Corneille, a young lawyer from Rouen, had a mild success with his comedy *Mélite*; but it was not until seven years and and four plays later that he produced the first great masterpiece of the century in *Le Cid*.

In the meantime Richelieu had been striving to show himself as great a dramatist as he was a statesman. In 1634, with five collaborators of whom Corneille was one, he had produced his *Comédie des Tuileries,* which had no success. Undeterred, he started on *L'Aveugle de Smyrne*. This time Corneille refused to work for him; and when this play also failed, and in January 1637 Corneille by himself produced *Le Cid,* a triumphant success from the first performance, the Cardinal had reason to be jealous.* It was not only that Corneille was succeeding where Richelieu had failed. *Le Cid* itself could be read as a defence of the duel, which Richelieu was vainly striving to stamp out; and it glorified Spanish valour and feats of arms, only six months after the "année de Corbie", when the Spaniards had got within seventy miles of Paris.

Richelieu for a time was persuaded to bow to the general high opinion of *Le Cid*. But he was not sorry when some of Corneille's rivals refused to do the same, particularly Mairet and a clique of writers from Le Mans. Georges de Scudéry, brother of the novelist, wrote some *Observations sur Le Cid* and, after Corneille had replied unrepentantly, challenged him to submit his work to the Academy and let them pronounce whether it was in line with Aristotle's rules for the drama.

* The evidence on this point is conflicting. Most contemporaries believed him to be furious; but he did not withdraw his protection from Corneille, allowed him to be ennobled, and took no action against the play or author except to force the Academy to pronounce on *Le Cid*.

"Les règles", and particularly the rule of the three unities, had been falsely deduced from Aristotle's *Poetics* in the Middle Ages—falsely because, although he urged unity of action (as all good dramatists have done), he only mentioned the unity of time as being current practice in his day, and he made no mention of the unity of place at all. But what Aristotle had meant as advice had been proclaimed as basic principles of dramatic art by Ronsard in his *Abrégé de l'art poétique* in the sixteenth century; and as the seventeenth century wore on, in spite of hair-splitting arguments as to whether "lucescit" in Terence meant dawn or first light, and therefore whether his *Heautontimoroumenos* lasted twelve or fifteen hours, the rules became more generally accepted and more rigidly applied. Corneille was to be their first victim—although, being a master, he was very often able to rise above them.

The "querelle du Cid", which finally got the Academy founded, lasted about a year. The Academy's first verdict was thought by Richelieu too favourable to Corneille; their second seemed too stern a condemnation. Finally they pronounced a verdict which satisfied neither side. Corneille retired to Rouen to think it over, decided to accept the Ronsard-Aristotle rules, and returned in 1640 with the two masterpieces *Horace* and *Cinna*. The Academy turned thankfully to other things, and notably to the preparation of its Dictionary.

This had been entrusted principally to Vaugelas, a literary nobleman who had lost all his money in the service of Gaston d'Orléans, and who was now commissioned by Richelieu to do the Academy's spadework. Progress was slow, and in fact Vaugelas died in 1650 and the Dictionary was not produced until 1694. But before Vaugelas died, he had published in 1647 his *Remarques sur la langue française,* a collection of notes which had far more influence on the development of French than the Dictionary ever had. He took as a criterion of good French what the best people at Court said and what the best writers wrote. "L'usage des gens du monde" was to be "le roi et le tyran" of the French language; and, from 1647 on, the language came under the discipline that was being applied to every side of French life—except the taxes. The work was so admirably done that French became the clearest and most perfect linguistic instrument in Europe, and remained the language of diplomacy until after the First World War.

It is important to remember that up to 1650 neither the language nor the literature had attained its classical perfection. Corneille himself never spoke French very correctly, according to a contemporary authority; and Voltaire wrote of him: "Mon père avait bu avec Corneille; il me disait que ce grand homme était le plus ennuyeux mortel qu'il eut jamais vu, et l'homme qui avait la conversation la plus basse." La Bruyère wrote of him: "Il prend un mot pour un autre, et il ne juge de la bonté de sa pièce que par l'argent qui lui en revient; il ne sait pas la réciter ni lire son écriture." He did not stick firmly to the rule of the unities either, allowing the action of a play to cover as much as thirty hours on occasion, even after his submission to the judgment of the Academy.

In 1659 Mlle de Trécesson, a maid-of-honour placed as a spy in the Court of the Princess of Savoy by Fouquet (whose name could be spelled either Foucquet or Fouquet) wrote to him: "Je ne pance qu'en vous, et touttes les amittiés que l'on me témoigne de part et d'auttre ne m'en détourne pas un momants." Young ladies' spelling is not always impeccable, but it is probable that hers was nothing out of the ordinary for those days, when the same name occurs in half a dozen different versions, sometimes even two of them in the same document. Discipline was on its way, but it had not yet been firmly or universally applied.

Nor, by 1650, had the philosophy which was to supply the background for the classical age been fully assimilated. But it had been thought out and written down. The last great name which belongs to this chapter is that of René Descartes, the author of the *Discours de la Méthode* (1637) and the *Traité des Passions* (1649). Descartes rejected all accepted authority in matters of philosophy, and admitted only what seemed impossible to deny. As this ruled out all impressions of the senses (because one's senses are often deceptive), all ideas (because one can have false ideas in dreams), and all mathematical propositions (because they can only be demonstrated by parallels), he was left with the one proposition which seemed to him quite certain—that he must exist, because he was capable of thought: "Je pense, donc je suis."

On this basis he built up a philosophic system, and while awaiting its completion he adopted his "morale provisoire", enshrined in four principles: to obey the laws and customs of his country, following the views furthest removed from excess; to be tenacious in the examination of even the most improbable opinions; to conquer himself rather than circumstances, and force himself to remember that we can control our thoughts more easily than anything else; and to spend his life in the cultivation of his reason.

Thus, behaviour was to be disciplined by "l'usage", just as the language was being subjected to the same "roi et tyran"; and those who are familiar with Corneille's work will at once recognize how Corneille's heroes and heroines demonstrate that "nothing is so easy for us to control as our thoughts." In his *Traité des Passions de l'Ame* Descartes maintained (on quite unsound scientific grounds, as we now know) that the blood, in circulating, carried the "humours" to the brain and back to the nerves and muscles; that the passions of the body thus affected the soul, which was linked to the body and particularly to a gland in the brain; and that not only did the bodily passions thus affect the soul, but they could, through this gland, be affected by the soul. "Our passions cannot be directly excited nor removed by the action of our will, but they can be indirectly controlled by thinking of things usually related to the passions which we wish to feel, and contrary to those which we wish to reject."

Descartes' philosophical and scientific ideas were rejected within a century, though his methods of logical analysis influenced French thought for far longer; but for his own age he had done two things. He had insisted that the use of reason was the only way to discover the truth (carefully excepting the truth in religion, which, being revealed, is beyond reason); and he had directed attention to the study of psychology. This belief in reason and the power of logical thought, and this application of reason to the study of men's passions, provided the philosophical doctrine which suited the century, and helped it to produce the tremendous character-studies which illuminate its literature.

Meanwhile the Academy continued its deliberations. It was consulted now and then by authors who wished to get its backing for their work. It ploughed on through the alphabet until at last the Dictionary was produced in 1694. It found a regular meeting-place in the house of the Chancellor Séguier in 1643, and in 1672 it was allotted its permanent quarters in the Louvre by Louis XIV. It never produced either its Rhetoric or its Poetics; and the Grammar which it finally produced in 1936 has had no authority whatever. The Academy's influence can perhaps be seen in the increasing devotion to the 'rules' of good literature in the second half of the century; but mercifully it never became that supreme arbiter of literary merit which Richelieu, with his passion for tidiness, clearly intended it to be. However, it did a great deal to raise the status of literary men in France; and the standing of an *Académicien* soon became such that in the next century we find Voltaire seeking election to the Academy in the hope of being sheltered thereby from censorship and persecution.

CHAPTER EIGHT

MOLIÈRE

IN THE year that King Louis XIII died, a young man called Jean-Baptiste Poquelin opened a theatre in Paris, which he christened the Illustre Théâtre. Since this is a political and social rather than a literary history, a whole chapter on the life of one man may seem out of place: but so much that is false has been invented about Molière, so many legends have become enshrined in Introductions to his work and literary text-books, that a historian of the period has a duty to correct where he can. Moreover, the life of Molière reveals much that is illuminating in the manners of the period: and his works reveal even more. To understand seventeenth-century France, one must read—or better, see—the plays of Molière; and to get the best out of them, one should know something of their author.

Jean-Baptiste was born in 1622, the eldest son of a draper and upholsterer successful enough to become *tapissier du roi* in 1631. This was an appointment which involved attendance on the Court for three months in each year, and although it did not involve paying the *paulette*, it was hereditary. The family must have been comfortably off.

Critics have tried to make out that after his mother's death in 1633 he suffered from a cruel stepmother. But his stepmother lived for only two years after her marriage, and during that time he was sent to the best school in Paris, the Jesuit Collège de Clermont. After five years there he studied law for eighteen months, and obtained a law degree from Orleans University. That, however, does not seem to have been difficult. His contemporary Perrault has described how he

(Perrault) and two friends suddenly decided one evening that they would take a degree at Orleans. So they rode down from Paris, arrived very late, woke the porter and told him what they wanted. The porter asked if they had the fees with them. They replied that they had, so he went off and fetched three Doctors of Laws, who appeared in cap and gown over nightcap and nightgown. Each asked two or three questions, and as Perrault answered them he jingled his money-bags; each answer was pronounced correct. Very soon they said they were satisfied, signed the necessary forms, and went back to bed, while Perrault and his friends went off to celebrate their degree in law!

Molière may have done much the same. At any rate, he never practised at the bar, though he did find time to translate long passages of Lucretius into French verse at this period of his life. He must already have been stage-struck, though: for by January 1643 he was ready to renounce the right to succeed his father as *tapissier du roi* (a right obtained for him six years before) in return for a payment of 630 *livres* "to be employed for the aforementioned purpose." The formal renunciation does not say what the purpose was: but it can only have been to set him up as an actor, since in June of the same year a legal deed constituted the Illustre Théâtre, with Poquelin and the beautiful Madeleine Béjart among the seven members of the troupe.

His father (falsely accused of cruelty to him in many of the text-books) could have prevented him from giving up his job in the firm until his legal majority at the age of twenty-five. On the contrary he helped him to get a start on the stage; and in September the new troupe hired a Real Tennis court (covered) in the Rue de Seine, and fitted it up as a theatre. In October they hired an orchestra of "trois violons", and after playing in Rouen (Corneille's native town) for a couple of months they settled down in Paris.

By June 1644 Poquelin's influence was already growing, for

in that month a new deed reconstituted the troupe, with him as its head. In this deed he formally took the name of Molière: why, no one knows; but it may well be that he found Poquelin too comic, since there is no question that he aspired to be a tragic actor. Most actors of the day seem to have had stage names, so there was nothing odd about Molière choosing one for himself.

Unfortunately the troupe was running into difficulties. In September they announced that they were under the patronage of Gaston d'Orléans, but they had to be lent 1100 *livres*: and a further 2000 were needed in December. They blamed it on the unfashionable neighbourhood where they were acting, and tried a move in January 1645 to another tennis court, in what is today the Quai des Célestins: but it did not work. In August 1645 the troupe collapsed, and Molière was imprisoned for a few days for debt, until his kindly father settled accounts for him.

From then till 1648 there is no certain trace of his whereabouts; but a clue is provided by the fact that Madeleine Béjart was acting in Bordeaux in 1646. There was a troupe of actors in Guyenne under the patronage of the Duc d'Épernon, led by an actor called Dufresne. Madeleine Béjart and Dufresne had acted together before. And as Molière's next appearance is in this troupe, it seems highly probable that after the collapse of the Illustre Théâtre, he and Madeleine went off to seek work with Dufresne in the provinces.

Anyway, on April 23rd, 1648 "le sieur de Morlière (*sic*) de la troupe Dufresne" asked permission of the aldermen of Nantes to perform in that city. From then on it is possible to follow their movements with fair accuracy from legal documents. In 1649 Dufresne was paid 75 *livres* for performing at Toulouse, and was refused permission to act at Poitiers "attendu la misère du temps et la cherté des blés." In 1650 Molière was godfather at a christening in Narbonne. And in the same year d'Épernon was recalled from his post as governor of Guyenne, and left the troupe flat. Molière then took it over from Dufresne. He was still only twenty-eight.

During all this time—and for most of the next eight years—he and his troupe led a wandering life. They would have to be constantly on the move, since there were few towns big enough to provide audiences for them for more than a few nights. The whole troupe, with its scenery, props and probably benches—and all its worldly goods—would be carted round in heavy wagons from place to place over terrible roads, stopping wherever there was the hope of an audience, even for a night. In some towns, as we have seen, they might not be allowed to act at all; in many they were unpopular (officially) because they were suspected of carrying diseases from place to place. The plague had not yet abandoned Europe; also, actors were still under the ban of the Church. It may have been a cheerful life, but it cannot have been an easy one.

In some villages they would find a barn or the courtyard of an inn to act in; in many towns the authorities would insist on their using the Town Hall, for which the town could charge a rent. Even if they used the Town Hall, if they were allowed to stay more than a week or so they were generally expected to give the proceeds of at least one night to charity. And if not taxed by having to use the municipal building, they might have to pay the town in some other way for the right to amuse it, as well as having to find and hire a hall big enough to hold a profitable audience—at ten *sous* a seat, or twenty for new plays.

One of the most satisfactory ways of making their living was to get a contract to act in the evenings before the Estates of the Province, when these were assembled. Dufresne's troupe had, in d'Épernon's day, performed at Agen before the Estates of Gascony. In 1650 Molière's troupe were paid 4000 *livres* for acting at Pézenas for three months for the Estates of Languedoc. In 1652 they again played for the Estates of

Languedoc, at Carcassonne this time. Later that year they moved up to Grenoble, and they spent the winter in Lyons, which must have given them a welcome rest from the hardships of winter travel.

1653 was a decisive year. In the first place, the troupe acquired two new members, the du Parc husband and wife, of whom the wife (though on the stage she called herself Mademoiselle) was a brilliant actress and a beautiful woman—a new star to succeed the ageing Madeleine Béjart. In the second place, the Prince de Conti was appointed Governor of Languedoc, and he brought with him a mistress who was extremely fond of the theatre.

Molière was tipped off by his secretary, and in competition with two other troupes he bid for Conti's patronage. All three troupes played for the Estates at La Grange, near Pézenas, and by a mixture of good acting and judicious bribery Molière won the day. The troupe now had an official patron, and could call itself the "troupe de M. le Prince de Conti": though, like d'Épernon, Conti preferred, when he could, to get it paid by the Province through a vote of the Estates, rather than have to pay his actors himself.

The next four years were spent acting in Pézenas, Montpellier, Lyons, Bordeaux, Béziers. Between October 1654 and February 1655, for instance, the troupe acted for the Estates of Languedoc, for which they were voted 5000 *livres*. And there was now a new side to Molière's activities, since he had begun to write, as well as act, produce and manage the troupe. Most of what he wrote was farces, though in 1652 he had written a full-length play, *L'Étourdi*. These farces do not seem to have been written out in full. They were more like scenarios which the actors filled out for themselves as they went along, with speeches, by-play and jokes of their own devising. For their performance Molière got a payment for author's rights which increased his income; and they were certainly popular, and increased his reputation.

In April 1657 Conti was converted from libertinism to religion by the Bishop of Aleth; and renouncing both his mistress and his actors, he went off to command an army in Italy. The troupe had to carry on as best it could, and that summer they moved as far north as Dijon. After wintering in Lyons and Grenoble, they tried an even bolder move. They were in Rouen in May 1658; and on October 24th they made their début in Paris, in the Salle des Gardes of the Louvre, before the King and Court, under the patronage of Monsieur, the King's brother. The play was Corneille's *Nicomède,* followed by one of Molière's farces, probably a sketch, now lost, called *Le Docteur Amoureux.* The tragedy had only a moderate success; but the King laughed at the farce.

The thirteen years in the provinces had changed and developed Molière. True, he was still a townsman above all, and there is never a hint of "wood-notes wild" about his work. Almost the only reference to nature to be found in a play of his is by Tircis in *Les Amants Magnifiques*:

> Silence, petits oiseaux,
> Vents, n'agitez nulle chose.
> Coulez doucement, ruisseaux,
> C'est Calliste qui repose.

—where he only seems to mention it in order to tell it to be quiet! In the same play he says:

La princesse passait presque seule dans la forêt par ces petites routes qui sont si agréables, lorsqu'un sanglier hideux (ces vilains sangliers font toujours du désordre, et l'on devrait les bannir des forêts bien policées); lors, dis-je, qu'un sanglier hideux est venu traverser la route où nous étions. Je devrais vous faire peut-être une description étendue pour orner mon récit, mais vous vous en passerez, s'il vous plaît.

There is nothing here but gentle satire on the pastoral adventures of the shepherds and shepherdesses of *Astrée*: and it is significant that the only time he accepted a commission to write a pastoral play himself, he never finished it.

What interested him was not nature, but mankind; in this respect he was a typical Frenchman of his century, which saw few charms in nature in the modern sense. And his wanderings had given him a wide acquaintance with Frenchmen of every class and kind, while his sympathy had allowed him to see them as human beings, and not merely as types or "humours." His wit had remained the caustic, 'cockney' wit of the capital, with a strong flavouring of the traditional low comedy still popular both in Paris and the provinces; but he had added to it an understanding of characters like M. de Pourceaugnac and la Comtesse d'Escarbagnas; and although he did not seem to realize it yet, he was ready to achieve a unique triumph, in that, as Professor Michaut says, "seul en France, il a su dans une même pièce nous faire rire de tous les rires." He had learned how to combine farce, social satire, comic situation and the comedy of caricature.

At first, though, he stuck to his ambition to become a tragic actor. In the first year his troupe performed twenty-one different plays, mostly tragedies. Unfortunately, his talents did not seem to lie in that direction; and he had all too powerful rivals.

When he returned to Paris, there were three companies of actors in the capital. There were the Italians, who acted in mime in the Palais Bourbon, and with whom Molière's troupe had to share a theatre for the first two years. The Italians took the 'good' nights—Tuesday, Friday and Sunday—and the Troupe de Monsieur had to make what they could out of the other nights until the Italians went home in 1660.

Then there was the Troupe du Marais, now declining and out of fashion. Molière soon stole from them their only remaining good actor, and as the centre of fashion moved ever westward, away from the Marais, they ceased to matter. But finally there was the Hôtel de Bourgogne, so well established that if you spoke of going to "the Theatre" without further explanation, it was assumed that you meant going to the Hôtel. The troupe there had the title of Troupe Royale; they had the exclusive privilege of announcing their plays on red play-bills; they had a regular pension of 1200 *livres* a year to rely on from the King; and, above all, they had an established tradition of fine tragic acting and declamation.

In vain Molière ridiculed them (as in *L'Impromptu de Versailles*) for stopping at the fine bits to let the audience know when to applaud, or for roaring like a devil instead of speaking humanly when acting a king having a private conversation with the Captain of his Guard:

> Molière (*sarcastically taking the part of himself at a rehearsal*): "Comment, vous appelez cela réciter? C'est se railler: il faut dire les choses avec emphase. Écoutez-moi. (*Il contrefait Montfleury, comédien de l'Hôtel de Bourgogne.*) Voyez-vous cette posture? Remarquez bien cela. Là, appuyez comme il faut le dernier vers. Voilà ce qui attire l'approbation et fait faire le brouhaha. —Mais, aurait répondu le comédien, il me semble qu'un roi qui s'entretient tout seul avec son capitaine des gardes parle un peu plus humainement, et ne prend pas ce ton démoniaque?—Vous ne savez ce que c'est: allez-vous-en réciter comme vous faites, vous verrez si vous ferez faire aucun Ah!"

It is clear that Molière, who insisted on nature being the model and who hated exaggeration, was all too prosaic to bring out the formal splendour of classical French poetry, even though the most highly polished of his own plays are written in verse. It soon became clear that if Molière wanted to make money, for his troupe as well as for himself, he must stick to comedy.

The most devastating proof of this—to anticipate for a moment—came in 1665. Molière had offered to produce a play for his young friend Racine—*Alexandre le Grand*. With only one play behind him, and no reputation as yet, Racine must have jumped at the offer, especially as he had seen, and was soon to fall in love with, Molière's star, the du Parc. Yet, on the night of the fourth performance, Molière discovered that the Hôtel de Bourgogne was also performing the play, and from that day on it was the Hôtel which produced all the works of France's greatest tragic writer.

Not even Racine could have injured and insulted Molière like this, after the kindness which the older man had shown him, if he had not felt strongly that his play was being murdered by Molière's troupe, and that its beauties would be brought out better by that of his rivals. And it was presumably the fault of Molière himself, since in the following year Racine paid tribute to the acting talents of Mlle du Parc by stealing her from the Palais Bourbon and taking her to the Hôtel de Bourgogne, to act the name-part in *Andromaque*.

Everything conspired to make Molière a comic playwright. After a year of moderate success in 1658-59, he produced the first of his masterpieces in *Les Précieuses Ridicules*. This little one-act play was so successful that it was put on forty-four times in a single year—a tremendous number for those days—besides being acted on 'visits', when the theatre would be closed and the whole troupe would go to Chantilly, St. Mandé, Vincennes or some other great house, to amuse the guests at a party given by Condé, Fouquet or the King himself.

It earned for Molière 1000 *livres* for author's rights; and his second Paris play, *Sganarelle*, earned him 1500. Soon he was so well established that he could charge double for first nights; and by the time that *Tartuffe* was produced, in 1669, the takings in the first twelve performances were never lower than 1300 *livres* for a single night—very different from a payment of 5000 *livres* for four months' acting down in Languedoc. After the success of *Sganarelle*, moreover, the King undertook to pay the troupe the pension promised, but never yet paid, by his young brother. So from 1660 onwards the whole troupe had a strong vested interest in forcing Molière to write more and more comedies, since the profits were divided up between them, and new comedies spelled higher profits.

Molière

All the theatrical troupes were what we should nowadays call co-operative repertory theatres. Each actor had a share in the theatre, and the leader or manager of the troupe had an extra share for his extra work. Molière made money steadily from now on, since he was not only the leading actor, but also the manager, the producer and the author of their most profitable plays, for which they voted him special payments. In spite of pirated editions, too, he must have made something from the published editions of his works. And he must have been extremely busy, with all these activities.

In 1662 he found time to get married: not, as his enemies vilely suggested, to his own illegitimate daughter, but to a much younger sister of his old friend Madeleine Béjart. Unfortunately, Armande Béjart was too much younger— twenty-three years younger than himself, in fact. She liked a gay life: he was a very busy man. The marriage was not a happy one, but there was no open breach, and he left his widow all his money at his death.

From 1669 on he was a sick man, and his peace of mind cannot have been increased by any faith in his doctors—several plays show all too clearly how low was his opinion of the medical men of his day. The irony of his death is well known: how he was carried off the stage in a paroxysm of coughing during the fourth performance of the play, *Le Malade Imaginaire*, in which he makes the most fun of doctors, and in which a doctor actually rounds on Argan, the character played by Molière himself, and says he hopes that within four days he will be dead. Within four days Molière was dead, and there were not wanting doctors to say it was a judgment on him. Nor did the Church relax its strictness in his favour. As an actor he was excommunicate, and he had to be buried at dead of night. The *Congrégation du Saint Sacrement* had succeeded, in spite of all the King could do, in getting the performance of *Tartuffe* banned between 1664 and 1669. He had triumphed over them

H

then, and once Louis had made a Concordat with the Pope and felt strong enough to override clerical opinion, *Tartuffe* was produced. Now the Church took its revenge on Molière's dead body.

He won a posthumous triumph over the Hôtel de Bourgogne, however. His troupe carried on for some time without him, and then after ten years Louis, with his love of tidiness and official control, amalgamated the two troupes into one. It was —and still is—officially called the Comédie Française. But it is also still referred to, not as the Hôtel de Bourgogne, but as the Maison de Molière.

CHAPTER NINE

1661

O N AUGUST 17TH, 1661 the young King Louis XIV was the guest of his *Surintendant des Finances*, Nicolas Fouquet, at the latter's wonderful new *château* of Vaux-le-Vicomte. It was an evening party, suitably symbolic, for after it the sun set on freedom of expression in France for fifty years.

The organization was in the hands of the great Vatel, not only a magnificent *chef de cuisine*, but the director of the whole huge household, in charge of all arrangements for food, entertainment, the parking of carriages, the staging of the play, the ordering and lighting of the fireworks. Vatel took his rank and duties so seriously that he finally, in 1672, ran himself through with his sword during another Royal visit, to Condé's *château* at Chantilly this time, because the supplies of fish for the dinner seemed to be running short, and he believed his reputation was lost.

Vaux-le-Vicomte, with its gardens, was the work of Le Nôtre, who afterwards laid out the park of Versailles. The first thing that happened at the party was that Louis was offered a magnificent portrait of himself by Lebrun, painted without His Majesty having given a single sitting. Among the train of Fouquet's gentlemen-in-waiting was a new poet, La Fontaine, whose work had recently won him a pension from the great *surintendant*, a liberal patron of all the arts.

There was less merit, perhaps, in his having picked on Molière to entertain his guests with a new play (*Les Fâcheux*, written and produced in a fortnight), since Molière was already well known. More noteworthy is the presence among his guests of his devoted friend and supporter Madame de Sévigné, already beginning to write her incomparable letters. It was a brilliant scene, with fountains playing everywhere, as they were later to play at Versailles, and a tremendous display of fireworks; and as the last rocket fell, the last Bengal flare which had lit the gardens flickered out, and Louis XIV's carriage rolled off in the night towards Fontainebleau, Fouquet may well have thought that the time and money lavished on it had been well spent. He must have felt certain that he would soon get the reward he coveted, and be named First Minister in succession to the dead Mazarin. Surely Louis must by now be tired of playing at being his own First Minister. . . .

But Fouquet had miscalculated completely. In the first place, he had utterly misunderstood Louis, who was quite determined to be his own First Minister to the end, and would brook no rivals. In the second place, he had grown so used to the financial methods employed by Mazarin that he could not change his ways, nor realize that a deadly enemy in Colbert was busy every day reporting to the King how much the *surintendant* was putting into his own pocket, and how little was reaching the King's Treasury. In the third place, he had rashly revealed to Mlle de la Vallière that he knew of her liaison with the King: a move by which he had hoped to be accepted as a sort of benevolent 'uncle' to the new mistress, but which, in fact, had shocked and horrified her, because (poor shy creature) she had desperately hoped that no one yet knew her secret.

She had hastened to tell Louis, who was furious. Only twenty-two, and not yet the cynic that he became in affairs of this kind, he felt that his beloved had been insulted. And by whom? By the man who had indeed kept a trickle of money flowing into the Treasury; but only by borrowing at usurer's rates and taking large commissions on the deal, by mortgaging the revenues in advance, so that in 1659 the entire revenue for 1660 had been pledged and some of 1661's as well, and by mixing up his private accounts and the public accounts so thoroughly that no one except himself knew where to look for the State accounts any longer, so that Fouquet's own personal credit seemed to be all that stood between France and bankruptcy.

This was the man, moreover, who had recently bought Belle-Ile to add to his lordships of Le Croisic, Concarneau and Guérande in Brittany; who was fortifying Belle-Ile with fifty cannons, and buying the title of "Viceroy of America" from the Marquis de Feuquières for 90,000 *livres*; who had acquired control of the whale-fishing *Compagnie du Nord* with its twenty-five to thirty armed vessels; who had bought six warships from Holland and placed them under his flagship *Le Grand Écureuil* (the squirrel was Fouquet's device, and his motto "Quo non ascendet", which did not help to endear him to the King). Louis did not need the "Plan of Defence", found later behind a mirror in Fouquet's house, to tell him that here was a man with a formidable concentration of power in his hands. No wonder that after the splendid evening at Vaux, paid for with the spoils of France's Treasury, while Fouquet was counting his chances of the First Ministry, Louis was actually commenting to the Queen Mother on the way home: "Madame, ne ferons-nous point rendre gorge à ces gens-là?"

Three weeks later Fouquet was in prison. He had been tricked into selling his office of *Procureur-Général du Parlement*, so that the *Parlement* (which was friendly to him) would not have the right to try him; and, true to the lessons of Richelieu, Louis had him tried by a special court. In spite of all fair and unfair pressure—Fouquet was allowed no lawyers to help him, nor was he even allowed to examine the papers on which the case was based—the trial lasted four years, and in the end Louis could not persuade the court to pronounce the death sentence. But as poor Fouquet—a rogue, undoubtedly, but a most attractive one—is taken off by Captain d'Artagnan (the real d'Artagnan, a courteous and distinguished Musketeer) to lifelong imprisonment, let us pause for a moment to see in what state he left France, and in what state Louis found it as he once and for all asserted his power, with that mixture of justice and injustice, cunning and patience, good sense and heavy-handedness which was typical of him.

First of all, vis-à-vis the rest of Europe France had now asserted her dominant position. By the Peace of the Pyrenees and the Treaty of Westphalia she had been admitted as an equal (at least) of the Empire and Spain. She had acquired, since Henri IV's day, Artois and Hainault, the three bishoprics and part of Flanders, Alsace and part of Lorraine, and in the south Cerdagne and Roussillon; and she only needed Franche-Comté and the rest of Alsace-Lorraine, Savoy, Nice and the tiny enclave of Orange to attain her twentieth-century frontiers.

She had a standing army of 150,000 men, and the two foremost generals in Europe, Condé and Turenne. She had a navy strong enough to police the Mediterranean, and capable of matching the British at sea, at any rate in the period of British neglect between 1660 and 1680. She had widespread if still struggling colonies, with trading posts in Canada, the Gulf of Mexico and India.

Her population was growing steadily, and was now about eighteen to twenty million, whereas that of Spain was actually declining—probably to six million in 1661—and the Empire had lost perhaps a quarter of its population between 1620 and 1650. England's population cannot have exceeded five million, and there were not more than two million Dutchmen in the rich little State on the Rhine delta. Italy and Germany were still only 'geographical expressions': what had France to fear from any quarter?

Henri IV had laid down the lines of progress: a compromise with Protestantism, a strong hand over the nobles, tidier administration and an alliance with Protestants abroad to defeat the Hapsburgs. These lines, dropped for a time by Marie de Medici, had been taken up again by Richelieu and (after the Frondes) carried through by Mazarin—with the modifications that the Protestants had had their political power taken away, and that the demands of foreign wars had disrupted the tidiness of the administration. In finance, both Richelieu and Mazarin had simply stated what money they needed, and ordered others to find it for them; Fouquet's real defence—only he was not allowed to use it—was that what he had done, he had done on Mazarin's orders. The result was temporary financial chaos; but it only needed a few years of peace and the tidy mind of a Colbert to make France rich again. Her fertile soil and industrious peasants only needed to be left alone to work.

Meanwhile society had been refined and disciplined, and women had acquired a new place in it as leaders of taste and inspirers of great artists. The language had been purified and new rules laid down for it. The taste for the arts had spread to the French Court, brought there by Mazarin, who had the most wonderful library (the foundation of the Bibliothèque Nationale) and the most fabulous collection of art treasures in Europe. His nearest rival was Fouquet himself; and Fouquet had the further distinction of having patronized many of the artists who were to give lustre to the reign of Louis XIV.

Of the great men of art and letters in France in the seventeenth century, Descartes was already dead, as were Vaugelas and Malherbe. Pascal had only one more year to live. Poussin had left the French Court for Rome, where he was to die within four years; Claude le Lorrain had already been famous for thirty years, and his best work was done; and Corneille also had produced all his greatest work and stopped writing for a time, though he returned to the stage a few years later.

Even of those whom we habitually associate with the reign

of the Roi Soleil, Le Nôtre, Lebrun and La Fontaine had, as we have seen, already been discovered and set to work by Fouquet. Molière had been given his chance in Paris by Monsieur, the King's brother, and had already written four of his best plays. The two Mansards were already at work on the completion of the Louvre. The first edition of de La Rochefoucauld's *Maximes* was nearly ready for the press. Madame de Sévigné, trained in the salons, had begun to write the letters which gave such pleasure that seventeen hundred of them have been treasured and preserved for us—and it was no thanks to Louis that she wrote them, since as a friend of Fouquet's she was *persona non grata* at Court after 1661.

Tradition has it that the dying Mazarin said to Louis: "Je vous laisse un grand trésor—Colbert." This remark, from the strictly historical point of view, is of very doubtful authenticity, as is Louis' alleged remark "L'État, c'est moi." But Colbert was in fact already there, trained and eager to do his work. So was Hugues de Lionne, the diplomat who shaped the French Foreign Service so efficiently that it became the model for all the other nations of Europe. So were the Le Telliers, father and son, Michel Le Tellier who had been Secretary for War since 1643, and his son, Louvois, Minister for War until the '80s.

In fact, only the names of Racine, Boileau, La Bruyère and Mme de La Fayette are missing from the list of those great artists who made the century so glorious for France; in the military world there was still Vauban to come, and in Church affairs Bossuet and Fénelon. By far the greater number were already active and well known, and Louis had only to reap the glory sown by his predecessors.

He must be given credit for recognizing the artists who were of the first rank, and for creating (for fifteen years or so) conditions in which they could do their best work. The ease with which Racine, for instance, achieved fame and fortune as a dramatist, stepping almost straight from his Jansenist seminary and his thoughts of taking orders into the first rank of European playwrights, was not only due to his own pre-eminent talents: it was also clear evidence of the favourable climate for artistic production created by Louis' example of splendid patronage, an example which was followed (for as long as they could afford it) by all the courtiers and great nobles.

But the glory did not last, and Louis failed completely to discover worthy successors to this first generation of great artists. He had been well trained, but he had little real taste; he mistook what was imposing for what was beautiful, and he followed a political course which soon made patronage financially difficult, if not impossible. And since for the next fifty-four years he insisted on being not only Prime Minister but also prime arbiter of taste and fashion, he riveted on France both political and artistic modes which were out of date before he had been twenty years on the throne. Neither art nor politics are static. Louis tried to make them so, and we have now to examine the causes of his failure.

CHAPTER TEN

LOUIS XIV—YOUTH AND GLORY

Louis' Youth

THE HEIR to all this harvest of glory, Louis XIV, was born in September 1638, the son, as we have seen, of parents who had been married twenty-three years and who had disliked each other for most of that time. He can hardly have known his father, who was ill, and often absent at the wars, during the five remaining years before he died. The boy was, however, devotedly attached to his mother, and also to the Cardinal, who was probably his mother's second husband.

It is hard to believe that he would have waited until he was twenty-three before taking over the reins of power if he had not been influenced by gratitude and affection towards Mazarin. He was certainly conscious very early of his station. When his father lay dying, he heard someone moving in his room, and called out to know who it was. "C'est moi, Louis XIV", came the answer; though the child was not yet five, and Louis XIII was not yet dead.

Education

His upbringing was, quite simply, as unwise as it could be. On the one hand he was offered flattery like this from his tutor: "You are the handsomest child in the world: you are the visible and authentic image of God." On the other he was only allowed six pairs of sheets in three years, so that his feet used to stick out through the holes. Perhaps this was what gave him the habit of sleeping with the bedclothes round his waist, and nothing but his nightshirt over his chest and shoulders, which he kept up until his last doctor, Fagon, made him sleep swathed in eiderdowns, in order to make him sweat.

His first copy-book taught him to write out: "L'hommage est dû aux rois: ils font ce qu'ils veulent." And so literally did his mother Anne of Austria take this that she used to encourage him to run away from his lessons and come and sit at her knee, particularly when she was engaged in the devotions which occupied an increasing part of her life.

In his early years, as Louis afterwards told Mme de Maintenon, his principal companion was the daughter of one of the maids. No one prevented him and his younger brother from hanging around the doors of the kitchens, stealing food from the trays as they passed; and he said that they would often grab a double handful of omelette and run away to consume it in some dark corner. Meanwhile, his formal education was so neglected that in later life he sometimes made the most absurd mistakes in public on matters of history or geography.

One of his tutors, Villeroy, was so obsequious that the boys nicknamed him "Marshal Oui-sire." The other, little Godeau, Bishop of Grasse, taught him lessons like this:

> The great and shining qualities which we see in all conquerors give them a claim on our esteem, although they make the world a desert. Wars are storms which serve to purge the earth, as tempests purge the air. Conquerors who depopulate the world are ministers of God. Widespread desolations, being periodic and fatal, have their reason and necessity; and if they meet us on their path, let us bow gratefully to the immutable decrees that order the world.

The Frondes

The next most dangerous influence on the formation of his character was the effect of the Frondes. These, for the young King, meant two flights from Paris, one in the night to the unfurnished Palace of Saint-Germain; they meant the mob jostling through the Louvre, insisting on seeing the boy Louis in bed, to make sure that he had not again left the capital; they meant several separations from the Cardinal whom his mother loved so well; they meant discomfort, distress, and often danger, for all around him.

As a result of all this, he determined on three things—two of which he would anyway have been advised to do by Mazarin. He was determined once and for all to reduce the nobles to obedience; to break the power of the *Parlement* and free himself from all constitutional fetters; and finally, to insulate himself from Paris, whose noisy, smelly mob had for three years made life so unpleasant for him. His neglect of the Louvre and construction of Versailles must have sprung slowly but directly from the worries of the Fronde years.

The Influence of Mazarin

Mazarin himself did two things for Louis. On the bad side, he kept the Treasury empty and his own coffers full, so that Louis, as we have seen, was often told that though he had no money himself he could always borrow some from the Cardinal. This must have rankled, and would help to explain his cruel behaviour towards Fouquet, and his determination at all times not merely to be, but also to show that he was, the richest man in the kingdom, and the one who could keep up the most splendid Court.

On the good side, Mazarin did more than people used to admit to train his Royal successor. In 1654 he started holding special sessions of the Council, at which only simple business was transacted and easy questions were discussed. The boy-king attended these, and was thus introduced to the business of governing without undue boredom or fatigue. A year or two later he began to attend all the Council sessions, whatever the business; and by 1657 he was encouraged to go round to Mazarin's room every morning when his work was over, where the old Cardinal would receive him *tête-à-tête*, and discuss the affairs of the kingdom with him for an hour or two hours, not allowing any outside interruptions, and passing on to him all his own vast store of statecraft.

Madame the Princess Palatine, Monsieur's second wife, who disliked Louis almost as much as she disliked her husband, and wrote a series of letters which are a mine of information on Louis' Court, pointed out that it was in Mazarin's interest to keep Louis ignorant of affairs in order to stay in power. But the boot was actually on the other foot. Louis may have been ignorant of history, but he had learned all that Mazarin could teach him about the art of ruling. It was Louis' gratitude and filial piety that kept Mazarin in power to the end of his life, not any ignorance of how to rule.

The Death of Mazarin

On March 8th, 1661, early in the morning, Louis was informed by his nurse (who apparently slept in the same room with him) that the Cardinal was dead. He dressed and locked himself in his study for two hours—possibly the only two hours that he ever spent alone in his whole life. He then met his heads of departments, and informed them that no major request was in future to be answered without his sanction, and no major decision to be communicated to his officials except over his own signature. Everyone thought this was a whim which would last a few months. It lasted fifty-four years.

Louis' Personal Rule

During the whole of that time he ruled with a mixture of industry, charm, self-control, and selfishness. He worked for eight hours every day, and more when business was urgent; and for most of the remaining hours he was on show, and could not relax. He knew exactly how to pay the kind of compliment that made his subjects loyal for life. "Cousin," he said to Condé as the Prince, crippled by gout, came limping up the stairs and apologized for his slowness, "one who moves under such a weight of laurels as yourself must needs move slowly." And when an aged nobleman announced that he was ruined and asked permission to leave Versailles, he was given a pension with the words: "You and I have known each other too long to separate at an age when neither of us can start looking for new friends. Do not desert me."

We have seen how he restrained his longing to be King indeed until the death of Mazarin. A more spectacular incident shows the same self-control. Lauzun, a courtier of few virtues and unbridled ambition, had been led to believe he was to be made Inspector General of the Artillery; but the post was given to someone else. Lauzun demanded an interview, and after an impassioned complaint, drew his sword and broke it, saying he would never serve such a King again. Louis, who loathed scenes anyway and who this time was entirely in the right, turned to the window, lifted his cane, and threw it out into the courtyard, saying: "J'aurais regretté de frapper un homme de qualité."

His selfishness is best shown by his treatment of those nearest to him. Early in his reign he used to make the Queen and the reigning mistress travel in the same coach together when the Court moved—and sometimes an ex-mistress and her supplanter were forced in together. And forty years later, when his favourite grandchild, the Duchesse de Bourgogne, was expecting a baby, he forced her, in spite of her prayer to be excused, to travel with the Court from Versailles to Fontaine-bleau, with the result that she miscarried, and the life of a possible heir to the throne was lost, not to speak of the danger to the mother.

Three Periods of the Reign

At first, however, it was not his selfishness that was noticed, but his charm. His personal reign falls into three periods, and there was little in the first of these to suggest what was to come later. The three periods correspond (very roughly) to the periods of influence of his three principal mistresses. The first, from 1660 to 1670, is the period of peace, splendour, and the affair with Louise de la Vallière. The second, from 1670 to 1685, is mainly the time of the influence of Madame de Montespan— a time of ostentatious brilliance and selfish aggression. From 1685 till 1715, with Madame de Maintenon at his side, Louis saw his country grow steadily poorer and weaker as a result of almost incessant wars; and even he, isolated as he was and surrounded by flatterers, must have felt how sadly his glory was diminished by the end of his reign.

The only real love affair in his life, in the fullest sense, was probably his passion for Mazarin's niece Marie Mancini, whom he really seems to have wanted to marry in 1658. Her uncle, however, was horrified at the idea, and rapidly separated them; Louis was made to understand that kings married for policy, not for love, and in 1659 he was married to the Infanta of Spain. She, alas for her, instantly fell in love with him; he courteously tolerated her, and in spite of his selfishness and open infidelity he was always formally polite to her, and often made her happy with a kind word or two.

Louise de la Vallière

But very soon he was flirting with Madame, Charles II's sister and his own brother's wife. To cover up their flirtation, which was probably never more than that, she suggested that he should pretend to be interested in one of her maids-of-honour, the awkward, shy, blonde Louise de la Vallière. Louis almost at once fell in love with her in fact, and Madame drops out of the story.

Madame de Montespan

Louise hated the publicity attendant on being the King's

avowed mistress; and in her unhappiness she confided more and more in her friend and attendant, Françoise de Rochechouart-Mortemart, Marquise de Montespan—a dark and beautiful creature of very different character from her own. The King met them together increasingly often; and in 1668 or 1669 the story repeated itself: Louise de la Vallière was abandoned (though forced for some years to stay at Court and watch her rival's triumph) and Madame de Montespan became the favourite. Wonderfully beautiful, as even her enemies admitted, witty, with excellent taste, it was she who for a time made the Court the most splendid in all French history. But she had a vile temper, and Louis was becoming more cynical and selfish as he grew older.

Madame de Maintenon

There were ruptures in 1672 and 1674, and the final breach came in 1680, after an affair which we shall examine later. Meanwhile she, too, had suggested her own successor. She had chosen as governess for her children by Louis (soon to be legitimized as "Children of France") a poor noblewoman of statuesque beauty and great discretion, the widow of the poet Scarron. Louis disliked this lady thoroughly at first, though he gave her the land necessary to make her Marquise de Maintenon, a rank sufficient for her post. And then, the more he saw of her, the more he came under her spell. In 1683, the Queen being dead and the Montespan having been finally dismissed, Louis almost certainly married his children's governess: from then on there is no mention of any other mistress.

First Period—Peace

During the first period of the reign there was only one war. True, as soon as he had assumed power he asserted his precedence over all other monarchs, and after squabbles by the French ambassadors in Rome and Madrid he forced both the

Pope and the King of Spain to accept the humiliation of public apologies. But neither of these incidents led to war. It was not until the death of Philip IV of Spain in 1667 that the troops of which he was so proud were used for anything more dangerous than colourful reviews before the ladies of the Court.

The War of Devolution, 1667

Philip had left two daughters by his first marriage, and a son by his second wife. The son succeeded at once to the Spanish throne; but Louis claimed that, in accordance with the law of Brabant, the daughter of a first marriage succeeded before the son of a second, and he at once invaded the Spanish Netherlands (which included several other provinces besides Brabant) in support of his wife's claim to the territory. It was not the last time that Louis was to twist the law to support his ambition.

He soon overran Franche-Comté in the east and the border fortresses in the north; but the Triple Alliance of England, Holland and Sweden was formed against him, and he decided to bide his time. He gave back Franche-Comté in return for being allowed to keep the fortresses of Lille, Charleroi and Tournai, and in 1668 peace was restored.

This war was a succession of easy triumphs, and since for once Louis knew when to stop, it only added to the glories of these early years. During the 1660's came the true splendour of the reign. Molière was at his best, producing at least two new plays a year. Racine made his début and wrote half his best works before 1671. In spite of his age, Corneille returned to the theatre, not in his finest form, but still capable of producing splendid echoes of the past. La Fontaine found his true *métier* as a writer of fables, the rebuilding of Versailles gave opportunities to architects, artists and landscape-gardeners, Boileau and Mme de Sévigné were exercising their very different talents. And above all, France was growing richer by the hour.

I

Colbert

This last was the work of Louis' great Minister, Colbert. On the arrest of Fouquet, Colbert took over control of finance and trade in France, and until 1671 his influence was paramount. Frenchmen regard him as greater than his predecessor Sully; but it is difficult to see any basic difference in their policies, except that Colbert attached more importance to industry and less to agriculture. Both insisted on honesty and tidiness in the administration; both saw the importance of better communications; both encouraged overseas trade; but neither of them saw the need for a radical reorganization of the 'system' of taxation.

Colbert cut down the *douanes* inside France by nearly three-quarters and thus made easier the movement of goods from one province to another. He improved the roads again, and he took up Sully's canal idea, constructing a network of waterways of which the most striking was the Canal du Languedoc, connecting the Atlantic with the Mediterranean. He encouraged manufactures, so that French silk, glass, lace and tapestry became the most famous in Europe. He did what he could (in the face of Louis' lack of interest) for colonial expansion and for the development of the navy.

In the countryside he insisted on a more careful and scientific exploitation of the royal forests, and set up a number of stud farms to improve the breeding of horses. But he believed that it was essential to ensure a supply of cheap corn, so he prohibited its export, which deprived France of a source of revenue and kept the farmers of the corn-growing areas poor, since France, then as now, produced more cereals than she needed for herself.

As a result of the ten years' peace, and of his honest and orderly accounting, plus new taxation on articles of luxury, Colbert was able to reduce the *taille* by half. But in order to protect his new industries, and to obtain a new source of revenue, he heavily increased the external Customs duties, and this led him into support of an aspect of Louis' policy which finally undid most of his own good work. The chief trading nation at this time was Holland: and the Dutch showed their resentment at Colbert's high tariff policy by putting heavy Customs duties on exported French goods. Colbert soon came to regard them as dangerous trade rivals and mortal enemies.

Second Period—The Glory

The Dutch War, 1672–78

Louis too, since the Triple Alliance, had regarded the Dutch as his personal enemies. They had, he thought, prevented him from adding to France most of modern Belgium. He was determined to be "glorious", and his idea of glory in a king was to add to the size of his territories, peacefully if possible, but if war was necessary, then by triumphant battles in which he could shine as a warrior. In this attitude he was supported by Louvois, his Minister for War, who was burning to show what his troops could do for their King; and by the nobles at the Court, who were beginning to realize that all posts in the public service were now barred to them, that the army was the only permitted alternative to Court life, and that war therefore provided their only opportunity for distinguishing themselves.

The Dutch War was a piece of cold-blooded aggression, carefully prepared by the whole of Louis' team. Louvois raised the army to 176,000 men; Colbert had filled the Treasury; de Lionne spent three years isolating the Dutch from their allies by adroit diplomacy. England was bought off by the Treaty of Dover, under which Charles II allowed himself to be bribed into neutrality; Sweden was likewise bribed, and the Emperor was frightened by a revolution in Hungary. On May 5th, 1672 all was ready, and Louis attacked from Maastricht and Liége at the head of 120,000 men, commanded, under himself, by Condé and Turenne.

At first, as in 1667, all went splendidly. Turenne—the planner, whereas Condé was the brilliant leader in battle—turned the Dutch line of defence on the Yssel, and Amsterdam lay open to the French. But Louis insisted on reducing all the Yssel forts before moving on the city, and this gave the Dutch time to open the dykes and flood the country. In the time thus gained they were able to reorganize their defence and awaken Europe to the danger of French aggression.

The Coalition against Louis

That winter Brandenburg and the Emperor joined the Dutch; in 1673 Spain and Lorraine came in against Louis; and in 1674 Denmark and the Elector Palatine strengthened the coalition. The war had become European, as the realization spread that it was no longer Spain that threatened to overrun the west, but the new, rich and unscrupulous power of France. To see the Dutch and Spaniards fighting on the same side was an astounding symptom of the way things had changed in Europe in the last twenty years.

The First Devastation of the Palatinate

Methods of war had not changed, though, in 1674 the first of two systematic devastations of the Palatinate by Louis' orders (the second was in 1689)—destruction of villages and vineyards, castles and crops—sowed the seeds of that Franco-German hatred which has persisted into the twentieth century. But in spite of such desperate measures, Louis could not make headway against so strong a coalition. Turenne, by now the greatest of his generals, was killed in 1675. Condé and Luxembourg carried on the war until 1678, but then Louis was forced to make peace.

The Peace of Nymwegen, 1678

At Nymwegen a peace treaty was signed by which France

gained Franche-Comté, which as usual she had easily overrun in the first campaign; but she gained nothing in the north, and indeed was forced to give up some of the territory which she had won from the Spanish Netherlands in 1668.

The year 1678 marks the turning-point of Louis' reign. Till then almost everything had gone well for him: from then on most things went wrong. The outward splendour remained, but the true glory steadily faded. He had already lost Turenne; and after 1678 Condé was too old for active soldiering. In the same way Molière had died in 1673, and Corneille had finally stopped writing plays in 1674; now Racine abandoned the stage in 1677, to become official King's Historian, and attend, whenever ordered, to read Louis to sleep with his beautiful reading voice.

In 1678 the last of the great masterpieces of the reign was published, Mme de La Fayette's *La Princesse de Clèves*; and by that year La Fontaine had published eleven of the twelve books of his *Fables*. Lebrun, it is true, carried on until 1688; and the Minister whose administration made it possible to pay for all this splendour, Colbert, did not retire till 1683. But once the Dutch war got out of hand, Colbert's views on policy had less and less influence. Money was needed more rapidly than he could produce it. Many of his proposed reforms were shelved. The tidiness which he had introduced into the Exchequer was disturbed again by the double strain of war and the building of Versailles. His rival, Louvois, Minister of Works as well as War, was listened to more and more. The huge private fortune which Colbert had amassed may have consoled him a little: but he died worn out, a disappointed and embittered man.

The rest of Louis' reign is a story of religious persecution and increasing poverty at home, continued land-grabbing and disastrous wars abroad, and in his personal life increasing rigidity, and boredom for those around him. The great harvest of glory which others had sown for him had been reaped by

1678; and he himself had not known how to sow for the future. There for the moment we will leave him, and examine the setting which he had made for himself, and the life and manners of those around him, before looking at the depressing details of his declining years.

CHAPTER ELEVEN

THE COURT AND THE COURTIER

WHEN LOUIS took over personal control of affairs, the Louvre was still his principal palace. The Court moved from there to Saint-Germain, to Fontainebleau, to Vincennes—cumbersome upheavals involving triumphs of organization in moving furniture, staff, etc.—but the hub of the circle round which it moved was still in Paris. As soon as he took over the reins, however, and had dealt with the business of Fouquet, Louis began to dream of a new palace which was to be his own especial monument. For this he chose his father's hunting lodge, some twelve miles from Paris at Versailles.

In 1624 Louis XIII had built for himself a small country house of brick and stone in the forest of Versailles, where he loved to hunt. A better king than his son, he had insisted that it should be paid for out of his "menus plaisirs" or private budget, so that it should not be a burden on the finances of the State. Between 1661 and 1668 this modest manor-house was transformed and extended, and Louis XIV spent more and more time there; it remained, however, a red and white 'Louis XIII' building, and it was still too small to serve the Court for more than a brief visit, such as the fortnight of the "Plaisirs de l'Ile Enchantée" in honour of la Vallière in 1664.

In 1669 Louis seems to have decided to abandon Paris for good, in spite of Colbert's remonstrances. He set in train a second reshaping of the *château*, this time to make it big enough to take his whole Court. He refused, however, to let his architects pull down the original "château de cartes", as Saint-

Simon calls it, and they had to envelop it on three sides only, keeping the King's bedroom as the centre—which is why part of the east side of the present palace is still in Louis XIII style, while the west is all in stone in the Classical style.

After 1671 he never lived in Paris; and in that year too he founded the town of Versailles, encouraging his nobles and Ministers to build their own houses there. But in spite of all this, the *château* still proved too small to be the permanent seat of the Government and the Court, and in 1682 he began a third rebuilding, extending it north and south with two great wings, and completing the *Galerie des Glaces*. Meanwhile work continued on the gardens, the canal was dug in the flat plain, the *Grand Trianon* was built (Louis was already finding burdensome the rigid etiquette he imposed in Versailles) and the *Orangerie* and stables were constructed.

The scale on which he was now working was colossal. In 1684, 22,000 men were at work, and in 1685 the number rose to 36,000. And yet it was not till 1710 that the final Chapel was completed—by which time Louis had really lost interest in Versailles, and was thinking of nothing but his new improvements at Marly. This was the spot, six or seven miles from Versailles, from which the water was pumped for the Versailles fountains and gardens. Here Louis (at a cost of 13,000,000 *livres*) built a charming little country house to which he could withdraw for a night or two of comparative relaxation, since it could only accommodate a few courtiers and Ministers, and the pompous ceremonial of Versailles was impossible. The wheel had come full circle. Marly was to Louis XIV much what Versailles had been to his father: but in the meanwhile he had saddled France with the largest white elephant ever seen, which had cost so much that he never dared to let the figures be published, and which, after being the centre of Europe for a hundred years, has been an empty and expensive monument to vanity ever since.

The fact that Louis cut himself and his Government off from the capital and the rest of the country was bad enough; but worse was that he completed the process, begun by Richelieu, of reducing all the nobility to the status of hangers-on at Court. Richelieu had encouraged them to leave their estates and live in Paris: Louis did his best to force them to leave even Paris and cluster round him at Versailles. He only gave favours and pensions to those who appeared regularly at Court, and had an eagle eye for an absentee. If any post or privilege were requested for someone who did not hang around the Palace servilely enough, Louis would frown and say, "Je ne le connais pas." Because of the scale of living he forced upon them, the posts and pensions were valuable if not essential; Vauban in his *Dîme Royale* estimates that by 1690 only one nobleman in ten was living on his own money. And even a royal nod or smile was useful; Louis knew that a few words from him to a courtier would stave off that courtier's creditors for another three or four months at least.

Louis also made life very unpleasant for any nobles who preferred to remain on their country estates. The *intendants*, never local men and always faithful servants of tyranny, would be ordered to harry them with heavy tax assessments, constant inquisitions and even (as in the case of Mme de Montespan's unfortunate husband) with trumped-up accusations. There were thus glittering prizes to be won at Court, even by nobles of very minor rank like Dangeau; and there was grave danger in staying in the country and incurring suspicion of sulking and plotting.

So many a country gentleman would set off for Versailles, having mortgaged his estates to provide him with an outfit and expense-money. There he would certainly find a great nobleman or two from his part of France, and the chances were that he would be related to one of them and could claim him as a patron. The nobleman would not refuse, for two strong reasons. One was the old tradition of surrounding oneself with pensioners, who increased a great man's feeling of self-importance; and the other was that a newcomer from the lesser nobility might well be in a position one day to repay the favours he had received. Louis never trusted the greater nobles enough to give them employment, except in the army; but many lesser men won important positions, sometimes for the most frivolous reasons, like Chamillart, who became a Minister because he was such a good billiards player that he became well known to the King at the baize tables; or Dangeau, whose gift for making impromptu verses earned him rooms in the Palace of Versailles itself, and a firm position in the royal favour; or Villeroy, who earned promotion by inventing a way of changing horses more quickly while hunting.

In Louis' younger days Court life was still fairly informal. In the early '60's Louis could still be pinched on the backside by Mlle de la Motte-Houdancourt so hard that he burst out with "Oh! la chienne!" at his mother's *lever*. At that time de Guiche could dare to set up as his rival for the affection of Louise de la Vallière, and Louis himself might be found with a party of young bloods climbing round the roof of the Louvre, looking to see if any maid-of-honour had left her window open.

But the older Louis got, the stricter the etiquette he imposed; he trained himself so hard to be kingly (as he understood it) that he gradually forgot how to be human. And since none of the courtiers were allowed to have any serious purpose in life, etiquette and precedence came to matter more than anything else to both the monarch and the men and women around him. It was fatal not to know the correct form: not to know, for instance, that inside Versailles itself you never knocked at a door, you scratched with a fingernail kept long for the purpose, and if no one came you went away; whereas in the town of Versailles you knocked at doors—once only at the houses of ladies of quality, more vigorously at lesser doors. No wonder that a nobleman with more sense than most remarked: "When I leave the Palace I often stop to watch a dog gnaw a bone, to remind myself that natural behaviour is still possible."

In the King's halls and salons conversation about politics was forbidden along with swearing and drunkenness. Louis did not like his nobles even to think or write about politics. After thirty years of service in the army, the great engineer Vauban came to the conclusion that all existing taxes should be scrapped in favour of a single "Royal Tithe" to be paid by everyone without exception. He set forth his argument in a book. Louis was so furious that he hardly spoke to him again. Vauban died soon after, broken-hearted at his disgrace; and Louis refused to pay any tribute to him even after his death.

As a result men's minds became narrowed, and great men who should have known better spent their time intriguing for the smallest favours and the silliest privileges. M. de Noyon, First Almoner and Bishop of Orleans, a man so pure, according to Saint-Simon, that no one dared risk an improper jest in his presence, and a bishop who spent six months of every year in his diocese—which was a lot for those days—quarrelled with his oldest friend and even with the King himself over a seat in chapel. There were four chairs behind the King, and he had got into the way of sitting in one which had been emptied by its occupant's death. In 1696 the King reproached de La Roche-foucauld (son of the author of the *Maximes*) for not attending the Lenten sermons. La Rochefoucauld replied that he did not intend to queue up for a seat, nor beg favours from an usher, nor sit among the lesser nobles; so Louis, who did not know what had been happening behind him, told him that he could have the vacant chair. The bishop, though an old friend of La Rochefoucauld's, was furious and withdrew to his diocese. Next year he came back to Court, but threw himself at Louis' feet in protest at the loss of his chair, saying that he could not bear the degradation of an office (First Almoner) which he had held for thirty-four years. Louis never changed his decisions, once announced; and at first he said crossly that if the decision lay between the bishop and a valet he would decide in favour of the valet. So the bishop retired again to Orleans. But Louis wanted to solve the problem, so in 1698 he first mollified the old man by appointing his nephew to the see of Metz, and then had a fifth chair placed for him in chapel, next to but below that of La Rouchefoucauld. On that basis they were all finally reconciled.

This de La Rochefoucauld, incidentally, though a man entirely without talent, became *Grand Maître de la Garde-Robe* and *Grand Veneur*. This meant that he had to attend the *lever*, the *coucher* and two other changes of the King's clothing every day. Three or four times a year he was allowed to dine in Paris; and just four times in the whole course of his life at Court he was allowed a few weeks' holiday.

The quarrels for precedence, of course, spilled over from the Court to the capital. When de Bouillon's second son was to read in public a thesis at the Sorbonne, where he was studying for the Church, the Duc de Coislin came in early, and took a seat some places down from the Princes of the Blood, in case a senior duke should arrive. Instead Novion, *Premier Président* of the Paris *Parlement*, came in and saw a chance to assert the *Parlement's* current claim to precedence over the dukes: so he took his seat above Coislin. The latter promply took his chair, planted it in Novion's lap and sat on it; and although the thesis had by now begun, he refused to get up until Condé had promised on behalf of Novion that the offence would not be repeated! Saint-Simon (a duke himself) reports this as the one creditable episode in a life "otherwise marred by excessive politeness": and all the Princes of the Blood paid visits of congratulation to Coislin next day.

Such instances of a false standard of values could be multiplied almost indefinitely, but they would become as tedious as the empty life which produced them. And it was not only tedious— it was remarkably uncomfortable. In spite of the immense building programme, there was never enough space to house the Court with what we should consider even a modicum of comfort or hygiene; and in spite of the grandeur of Versailles, it was too hot in summer and bitterly cold in winter. In hot weather the lack of ventilation and drainage made the place smell abominably: the slops and refuse were simply thrown out into the courtyards, and eighty years later Marie-Antoinette narrowly escaped a ducking from the slops thrown from Mme du Barry's windows.

In winter there were draughts everywhere, and courtiers were often hard put to it to live up to Louis' rather surprising standard for a gentleman: "Un homme de qualité doit pouvoir supporter la chaleur et le froid, la fatigue et la faim sans se plaindre." Twice in the reign the wine froze on the King's own table. But Louis can rarely have tasted hot food at any time after the move to Versailles. Before each of his meals the *maître d'hôtel* and the Clerk of Office had to go to the kitchens, wash, and dip two pieces of bread in every dish, one of which was eaten by the *maître d'hôtel* and the other by the equerry. Then the *Cortège de la Viande du Roi* was assembled, consisting of two Life Guards and an usher in front, then the *maître d'hôtel* and a gentleman servant and the Comptroller-General of the Household, then the dinner and finally more Guards. They crossed the street from the kitchens—and if anyone met them he had to take off his hat and bow as if to the King himself—then crossed a courtyard, and finally passed through several rooms to the King's table. There was a primitive hot-plate, but the food cannot have stayed hot through all this performance.

The presence of the Comptroller-General seems odd, and was presumably to ensure that nothing was stolen. Many things were, even from Versailles. The silver fringes off the curtains were taken one night and nothing could be discovered about the theft, nor ever was; but a few days later, while the King was at supper, a parcel suddenly landed on the table containing the fringes and a note saying, "Reprenez vos franges d'argent. La farce ne vaut pas le risque." On another night, in 1687, about £10,000 worth of harness was stolen from the stables. Some people were not too over-awed even by the majesty of Louis.

To return to the accommodation, most poorer nobles could not live in the Palace at all, but had to find quarters in the town. Only if you were 'lucky' like Dangeau did you get rooms in the *château*. Whether it really was lucky seems open to doubt. Saint-Simon had one of the best suites—so good that princesses used to borrow it for parties—and it only consisted of three small rooms, a hall, and two windowless closets. Less important people were much worse off. A lady-in-waiting would have to share a room even if married, and the partitions between the rooms were so thin that all conversations could be heard through them.

Life started early in the morning. Lesser fry would first have to attend the *lever* of their patron, and then he and his hangers-on would move off to attend the King's *lever*. This, according to Saint-Simon, was at eight o'clock, but, according to a gazette of the reign, it took place at 8.45. By then the First *Valet de Chambre*, who slept in the King's room, would have risen and put away his folding bed; the fire was lit, the Royal watch was wound up and two wigs were brought—a dressing-wig and a full one for the day. At 8.0 (or 8.45) the Valet would wake the King (though one suspects he must have been awake in fact before now), and as long as she lived Louis' Nurse would appear to bid him good-morning. The First Physician and First Surgeon came to rub him down and change his shirt (particularly necessary later in the reign, when Fagon prescribed sleeping swaddled in eiderdowns).

At 8.15 (or 9.0) the Grand Chamberlain entered with those nobles who had the *grandes entrées*, and with Holy Water: and Louis must have been a fine-tempered man at that hour, since this was found to be a good time to ask him for favours. The *grandes entrées* then withdrew again, and he recited the Office of the Holy Spirit. Next he put on dressing-gown and wig, and the *petites entrées* were allowed in to see him pull on his trousers and stockings, "which he did with extreme grace and very cleverly", as one witness recorded! The senior person present was then given the shirt by the First Valet to hand to the King, and Louis rubbed his hands and perhaps his face on a cloth dipped in alcohol. Every other day he was shaved. Baths, when he took them, seem to have occurred in the evening, with an official of the fifth section of the First Kitchen standing by with burning incense. The same section of Louis' five hundred personal servants included, incidentally, the two *porte-chaise d'affaires*, who had the privilege (for which they had paid) of emptying the royal commode.

Louis next took a cup of wine and water, or of sage-tea, and then knelt to say his prayers. Any clergy who were present knelt with him, while other courtiers remained standing. When he had finished, the King withdrew with his Ministers and senior courtiers to his private room, to arrange the programme for the day; and after that he attended Mass, and expected his courtiers to attend too, although they behaved extremely badly—in 1706 Marshal Boufflers one day laughed so loudly in the middle of Mass that the King turned round in astonishment to see what was going on. On another occasion the Captain of the Guard announced that the King was not coming, and ordered all the Guards to retire. The courtiers promptly retired too, all but a few; whereupon the Captain of the Guard got his men back just in time, and the King arrived to see with amazement an almost empty Chapel.

From about 10.0 A.M. till 1.0 P.M. there were Council

meetings, except on Thursdays, when Louis gave private audiences, and on Fridays, when he went to Confession. Meanwhile the courtier would try to get his dinner. Some people dined at 11.0, others at noon, and if he could not get a place with a friend or patron at either session, the needy courtier might find a seat among the Gentlemen Servitors, the five hundred for whom Louis kept a special kitchen. At 1.0 P.M. he could watch the King dine if he dined "au public" (when anyone could drive out from Paris to watch him) or "au petit couvert" (when all courtiers could be present). The King sat alone for this meal, unless Monsieur was present to sit with him: even the Dauphin was not offered a seat, and there were no ladies present.

In the afternoon there might be another Council meeting, or the King might go hunting. He was an extremely keen hunter and a good shot; and as there were about five hundred couple of hounds in the kennels, including Louis' staghounds, the Dauphin's wolf-hounds and the packs of the Duc du Maine and the Comte de Toulouse, there was plenty of hunting done. At Fontainebleau, in fact, the second Madame was delighted to find that she could hunt seven days a week. As Louis grew older he would follow the chase in a specially built light carriage: or else he would go for a walk in the gardens to look at his latest fountain—a penance for those who went with him, according to Madame, since he was a good walker, and she says that no one else at Versailles could walk two steps without panting and sweating—they were so fat and overdressed!

After exercise Louis would retire to work again with the Ministers, to chat with the current mistress, or later in the reign to visit Madame de Maintenon and often receive his Ministers in her rooms. Three times a week there was an *appartement* to entertain the Court—a concert followed by billiards or cards. The King might look in, and if he noticed any frequent absentees he would remark that he found it "fort mauvais"

The Louvre: a contemporary engraving

Madame de Maintenon and the Ladies of Saint-Cyr, 1686

that they should not attend. One advantage of the card-games was that they allowed the weary courtier to sit: otherwise he or she had to stand. Madame once reproved a duchess for sitting down when she was not playing, and the duchess left the Court for good.

Gambling was for high stakes, though some people openly cheated. D'Antin once confessed to having won 28,000 *livres* at a session, and Madame de Montespan lost 160,000 in an evening—but insisted on going on playing until she had won most of it back again. It was all in keeping with the spirit of life at Court, which for many was a gamble at all times; and anyway, for twenty years in the middle of the reign it was almost the only alternative to gossip. In the early years plays and ballets had frequently been offered; but as Louis grew older and stricter the "comédie" was stopped, until the arrival of his charming and lively granddaughter, the Duchesse de Bourgogne, persuaded him to start it up again. Thereafter, until the tragedies of his last few years, there was a "comédie" two or three times a week.

Supper-time for the King was officially 10.0 P.M., but it might be as late as 11.30 before he sat down to it. It was always eaten "au grand couvert" in the presence of the whole Court, with all those entitled to it seated at the King's table, including the ladies. But it was a gloomy meal, since Louis was too busy eating to talk, and no one else dared to say much when the Monarch was silent and the whole Court was watching.

Then the business of the *coucher* began. First Louis stood to receive the curtseys of the ladies; then he withdrew to his private rooms to spend up to an hour with his family—ladies seated, men standing throughout. Next he singled out a favoured courtier to hold the candlestick during the *grand coucher*, and in the candle-light undressed and dismissed the Court. But there was still the *petit coucher*, at which the elect could watch him sit ("pour la forme" only, apparently) on his

K

commode, and those who had the *entrée* could again ask for favours.

And at last—about 1 A.M.—the last of the weary courtiers could go to bed too. How many of them, one wonders, as they made their way back to a cramped lodging in town or palace, regretted the estates they had abandoned for this glittering, empty life, and yearned for the sane round of country pleasures and occupations, which they had sacrificed for a stake in the Versailles lottery?

CHAPTER TWELVE

THE POISONING SCANDAL

LIFE AT Court may often have been dull, but it was outwardly brilliant. Life in Paris, more free and easy and untrammelled by etiquette, was losing some of its sparkle as the centre of fashion and display moved out to Versailles. And simmering underneath the surface of both Court and City there was an almost literal witches' brew of horror, which was revealed by the hearings of the *Chambre Ardente* in 1679–80.

For all the glittering display, and the undoubted progress in arts and sciences, the public of the seventeenth century was still remarkably credulous. Belief in sorcery was still an article of faith—the great Churchman Bossuet believed in it, and a book by Jean Wier casting doubt on it found no adherents. Alchemists were still at work, trying to find the philosopher's stone which would turn everything into gold; astrologers preached to an even wider public than to-day. As late as 1687 a certain Pierre Hoque, a peasant, was condemned to the galleys for having cast a spell on the beasts of his neighbour Eustache Visée. The animals, however, continued to die even after his trial, so Hoque was persuaded to send a message from his galley to two shepherds, who alone, he said, could lift the spell. After he had sent it, he suddenly cried out that the lifting of the spell would cause his death—and die he did, in convulsions, "at the very moment", according to his judges, "when the shepherds were pronouncing the words which lifted the spell."

Witchcraft took on many forms of activity, and in Paris the

practice of palmistry and crystal-gazing was used as a cover for selling love-philtres, getting rid of unwanted children, and removing husbands or lovers who had become tiresome. The sorceresses gained enormous sums, as we shall see, and one of them said at her trial that they all earned far more from their hidden activities than they could ever have done by mere fortune-telling, and that poisoning was the most lucrative branch of their profession, bringing in as much as 10,000 *livres* per victim.

Everyone went to the fortune-tellers—it was the smart thing to do. Some did it in all innocence. But as soon as the "pythonesse" (as La Fontaine calls her) observed from a client's reaction that there was a difficulty over a love affair or an inheritance, she would offer her more sinister services: and even the highest in the land did not, apparently, hesitate to accept them. The Marquise de Lusignan was in La Voisin's house when she was arrested; the Comtesse de Soissons fled from Paris when the case came up. The Duchesse de Bouillon admitted having been to see her, but perhaps she had not been a serious client, since she had taken her husband with her. Even Racine's name was mentioned. He had certainly known La Voisin, and she accused him of having poisoned his mistress, the actress Mlle du Parc. We do not know that anything was proved against him, but he had certainly been moving in a more than doubtful milieu round 1670.

The Brinvilliers Affair

But before the main drama opened there was a curtain-raiser. In 1672 a certain Chevalier de Sainte-Croix died, and as he was in debt the justices sealed up his rooms and his possessions. When the Clerk of the Court opened them, he found a long envelope with a statement on the outside that it was a Confession. This he destroyed unread, because it was held that the confession of a dying man was as inviolably secret as if it had been made to a priest. He had also, however, left a *cassette* containing a number of bottles, with a letter saying that they were the property of his mistress, the Marquise de Brinvilliers.

This lady had already shown great nervousness, and demanded permission of the justices to recover her property from Sainte-Croix's rooms. When this aroused suspicion, and her request was refused, she gave herself away by fleeing to England. The French then demanded her extradition, and Charles II granted it, but on condition that the French carried out the arrest themselves, which gave her the chance to slip away to the Netherlands. Eventually she was arrested in Liége, and brought to Paris for trial: and the most extraordinary story was revealed.

In 1666, taught by her lover, who had the recipe from a Swiss chemist called Glaser, the Marquise de Brinvilliers—a great beauty, and a woman of rank and fashion, daughter of a high legal officer who was a *conseiller* of the Paris *Parlement*—had started experimenting with the use of arsenic. She had begun by visiting the public hospitals, where she distributed food, some of which was poisoned. When she thought she had the dosage right after these experiments, she started to poison her father, because her rank, she thought, demanded a scale of living which her husband's fortune by itself could not provide.

In fact it took her eight months to kill her father; and during all that time she nursed him with apparent devotion. Finally he died, and she inherited some money; but not enough for her and her lover, and by 1670 she was in straits again. So she then placed a certain La Chaussée (who afterwards gave evidence against her) as a footman in her brothers' house, and started to poison them. One brother died after three months' illness early in 1670; the other brother she also killed off, in September 1670. The fact that they had been poisoned was soon known, but no one could guess who was the criminal.

Her sister-in-law had some suspicions, however, so the

Marquise started to poison her. She also gave her own daughter poison when in a rage with her "stupidity" one day, but repented immediately and gave her an emetic. She had a fantastic temper, and once, when forced to sell a house to pay some debts, she was so furious that she rushed off after the sale and set fire to the house, to prevent the "honour of her family" being smirched by a forced sale of their property.

Her children's tutor, Briancourt, knew what she was doing and tried to denounce her, but no one would believe him; and she then tried to assassinate him by getting her lover to stab him after she had seduced him. He was too suspicious to let himself be seduced, and ran from the room when Sainte-Croix appeared. Then she tried poisoning her husband, but her lover Sainte-Croix preferred not to be left in command of the field, and gave him antidotes! After some months of this Sainte-Croix died, and the truth gradually came out.

The Marquise was questioned, tortured and finally induced to confess by a chaplain in the prison. She died bravely, looking so saintly that many in the crowd declared that she was in fact a saint, and rushed to get bits of her clothing, or to dip their handkerchiefs in her blood. Madame de Sévigné gives a vivid picture of her last hours in 1676.

Marie Bosse

Now this fantastic affair—though the Marquise had worked as a free-lance, so to speak, using "la recette de Glaser" for herself—had made people excited and suspicious. Poison was in the air, especially since the peritonitis which killed Madame (Henrietta of England) in 1670 had been widely, though wrongly, attributed to poison. Two years after the death of La Brinvilliers, a certain Maître Perrin, dining with Mme Vigoureux, heard a fortune-teller called Marie Bosse (who was very drunk) say: "Encore trois empoisonnements et je prends ma retraite, fortune faite." He might have thought it was a joke if he had not noticed how quickly his hostess silenced her talkative guest.

Perrin told Desgrez, the police officer who had arrested the Marquise de Brinvilliers, and Desgrez got one of his men to send his wife round to see Marie Bosse, with a story of wanting to poison her husband. The wife returned with a phial of poison, and Marie Bosse was promptly arrested—this was in January 1679.

La Voisin

From what she revealed it was possible to make other arrests, and notably that of La Voisin in March 1679. This was a fantastically horrible woman, the most extraordinary and infamous of them all. She had taken to fortune-telling and less innocent pursuits because her husband was out of a job; and for seventeen years she had supported ten people on her earnings, including her old mother. She was a devout and practising Catholic, and never missed Mass even though she celebrated Black Masses. She always took care to have children born in her house baptized: yet she claimed to have murdered 2500 of them, and either burned their bodies or buried them in her garden. (This figure may seem fantastic, but it was claimed that the fortune-tellers between them made away with as many as 400 unwanted babies a year.)

The Chambre Ardente, 1679–81

When it was seen that poisoning was widespread, Louis set up a special court to deal with it, which, from the colour of the hangings in the room where it sat, was called the *Chambre Ardente*. He put in charge of the hearings the very fine Lieutenant of the Paris Police, Nicolas de la Reynie. The court sat in secret (fortunately for Louis, as it turned out). This was not because of any desire to spare the accused, but because everyone believed in witchcraft, and it was thought that if the hearings were public, the people at large would learn how to practise the black art.

The court met 210 times, examined 442 defendants, and condemned 218 of them. Thirty-six were executed, two died in prison, five were sent to the galleys and twenty-three banished: the scandal was indeed widespread. But full justice was not done. The most guilty were too important to be punished, and even among the less outstanding criminals the standards of the day caused the court to discriminate.

For instance, a certain Mme de Dreux had poisoned any rivals for the favours of her lover M. de Richelieu, and had tried to poison her husband and Mme de Richelieu. But she was a cousin of two of the judges, and so, having appeared in court flanked by her husband and her lover, who pleaded for her side by side, she was let off. She immediately went off to another poisoner, was arrested again and banished; but the King allowed her to remain in France provided that she lived with her husband.

On the other hand Mme Brunet, who had fallen in love with de Rébillé, one of Louis' flute-players, had been horrified at her husband's suggestion that de Rébillé should marry their daughter, had poisoned her husband and married the flautist herself. As she had no important relatives, she was condemned and executed. Louis advised his flautist to leave the country if he was guilty, but de Rébillé, a man of honour with a clear conscience, gave himself up, stood his trial and was acquitted.

Nicolas de la Reynie

De la Reynie was a very fine man. Saint-Simon—no easy flatterer—says of him that "at the age of eighty he obtained permission to retire from his post of Lieutenant of Police, which he had been the first to ennoble by the justice, the modesty and the impartiality with which he had carried out his duties, without ever failing in their punctual performance, nor doing harm except as rarely and as little as possible: he was a man of exceptional virtue and great capacity."

He became very unpopular with the nobility, both *d'épée* and *de robe*, for his energy in following up the poisoners; it was said that the fact that la Reynie was still alive was proof positive that there were no poisoners! And after a time Louis, who at first had urged him to use the utmost zeal, suddenly took fright, and tried to hush things up. Colbert and Louvois demanded that witnesses be heard quickly and without fuss, and that prisoners be spared the torture, so that only minor matters would be revealed. After a tremendous struggle with his conscience, la Reynie refused to allow such a travesty of justice: so the court was closed in October 1680. In 1681, how-ever, la Reynie had four interviews with the King, and persuaded him to re-open it; but the Lieutenant found himself hampered at every turn. Finally he suggested in despair that the only solution was to imprison all suspects by *lettre de cachet*, and close the court. Two unimportant wretches were executed to give a final semblance of activity, and then la Reynie's suggestion was carried out, and the court was closed in July 1682.

Madame de Montespan

The reason for Louis' change of heart was simple—and terrifying. He had learned that Mme de Montespan was deeply involved. La Voisin had been executed without mentioning her, but it was remembered later that she had hurriedly confessed to a number of horrid crimes, and yet had seemed afraid that something worse would come out. The something worse was no less than the attempted poisoning of Louis himself, and what she had feared was the ghastly penalty for regicide.

But another poisoner, La Filastre, revealed the secret, and from then on witness after witness confirmed it. Mme de

Montespan, it appeared, had had diabolic prayers recited over her head in order to win the King's favour as early as 1667. These prayers, astonishingly, seemed successful, and in 1668 she was bold enough to have Marietta and Le Sage, her diabolists, come to Court at Saint-Germain to say more 'prayers' for her. They were arrested on suspicion of sorcery, but although they confessed why they had come, and Mme de Montespan fled the Court for a time, the King made light of the affair and hushed it up.

That scandal blew over: but when in 1672 she fell out of favour with Louis for a time, she went to La Voisin, and this evil woman, with an unfrocked priest called Guibourg, recited Black Masses for her. These—there had to be three of them to be effective—involved the sacrifice of a child, while the Mass was recited backwards over the body of the King's mistress, and the child's blood was drunk by Guibourg from the devil's chalice. No wonder that Louis was horror-stricken when he learned of it. The woman who had been his mistress at intervals for ten years, who had borne him four children, the brilliant creature who had been the centre of his Court, had depraved herself in this appalling way. Moreover, he had himself suffered from giddiness and headaches in 1672: and La Voisin's daughter deposed that in that year she had several times taken love-powders from her mother to Versailles for Mme de Montespan to give to the King.

In 1676 the favourite was again afraid she was losing her hold on Louis, and again she turned to La Voisin. This time she said that she could only attend one Mass herself, but La Voisin conscientiously performed the other two, apparently quite convinced of their efficacy. And in 1679, when the King's favour seemed to be turning towards Mlle de Fontanges, La Voisin accepted an offer of 100,000 *livres* to poison the King himself.

She proposed to do it by handing the King a *placet*—a

written plea for mercy—in favour of an imprisoned criminal; inside the *placet* was a charmed powder which would kill Louis on the spot. One Thursday in March 1679—on Thursday mornings the King received such *placets* at the Court—she went to Saint-Germain; but the King did not appear in person, and she refused to offer it to an underling, because he would then open it first. She returned home vowing that she would go again to Saint-Germain; but next day she was visited by the "Missionaries" of St. Vincent de Paul (unbeneficed clergy who worked among the poor and the criminals of Paris), who sensed that something was badly amiss in the household and denounced her. She burned the poisoned *placet,* but on March 12th she was arrested on suspicion.

Even after this Mme de Montespan tried to get Mlle de Fontanges murdered—having herself left the Court hurriedly on March 15th. She was unsuccessful: and there we can leave her, remembering only that this was the woman who brought Louis' Court to the highest pitch of brilliance. It is a reminder that the horrors and splendours of the Italian Renaissance were still, in 1670, not so far in the past, and that the so 'civilized' aristocrats of France were often darkly human underneath.

Louis' Injustice

The person who comes worst out of the affair is Louis himself. At first all eagerness to root out the criminals and see justice done, as soon as the scandal came so close to home he reversed his policy and did his utmost to hush it up. He ordered all depositions implicating Mme de Montespan to be separated from the rest, and later (in 1709) burned them with his own hands. If it were not for la Reynie's own notes, hurriedly made at the time on the covers of the dossiers, the truth would not now be known. Even as it is we are left in ignorance about the most interesting person involved, though it is probable that he was only involved accidentally.

Racine was deeply in love with the actress Mlle du Parc. In 1669 she died suddenly; and La Voisin, who knew her, deposed that she could have saved her, but was kept away from her by Racine. This would in fact point to a desire on Racine's part to protect his mistress from the evil old woman, rather than to any more sinister implication, but there are two pieces of negative evidence which are nonetheless intriguing. One is that Racine's dossier was one of those extracted from the files and handed to Louis personally, and the other is that in 1679, at the moment when the scandal burst, Racine, who had already withdrawn from the stage in 1678 and made his peace with the Church, now accepted the post (for which he was unbelievably ill-suited) of "Historiographe du Roi." He was to spend his time writing up the King's feats of arms in verse. Louis may have thought this a fitting occupation for the greatest poet of his age—this, and reading His Majesty to sleep! But Racine himself must have known better, and it looks uncommonly like the old fable of the flea taking refuge in the dog's armpit: in an official position close to the King Racine felt himself safe from attack.

And it must not be thought that if Racine had been guilty Louis would not have kept him at Court. Although Louis said, when he heard of Mme de Montespan's death, "du moment que je l'ai congédiée elle était morte pour moi," she in fact stayed at Court until 1691, and she only died (terrified, with her women round her night and day, and lights on even when she slept) in 1707.

She was more fortunate than many less guilty people—more fortunate indeed than several innocent ones. All prisoners who knew about her part in the scandal, whether guilty or innocent of crimes themselves, were imprisoned for life. The last survivor of them died in 1724. Several were guilty of nothing except having been in prison with those who knew the inner story, and who might therefore have told them about it. But Louis wanted the scandal buried; and Louvois was only too anxious to play up to his royal master. He had these unfortunates divided up into small groups and scattered about the prisons of the country, and there they remained, the innocent chained next to the guilty, till death came to set them free.

Louis' part in the whole business is despicable, even by the standards of his own day, and although it is true that from 1682 date his conversion, his abandonment of his loose way of living and his increasing devotion to religion, even that cannot be counted wholly to his credit. Racine and Mme de Montespan at least devoted a great part of the rest of their lives to good works: but Louis' idea of good works, as we shall see in the next chapter, was to begin a period of religious persecution which is one of the most unpleasant features of his reign.

One is almost glad to note that the affair recoiled on him in a curious way. The Comtesse de Soissons, Princess of Savoie-Carignan (born Olympe Mancini, niece of Mazarin) was compromised and fled into exile with her son Eugène. When he grew up she begged Louis to take him into his service: Louis refused. So Prince Eugène of Savoy took service in the army of the Emperor, and became, after Marlborough, the ablest of the Allied generals who inflicted so many defeats on Louis in his later years.

CHAPTER THIRTEEN

LOUIS XIV—THE DECLINE

Louis had been thoroughly scared by the revelations of the *Chambre Ardente*. He was, moreover, just past the age of forty, an age at which men are apt to put aside the follies and splendours of youth, and to settle down into a more careful middle age, or even, as happened to Louis, to harden into a rigidity of mind which turns more and more towards despotism. He had had twenty years of power and flattery to spoil him by now; and he had fallen under the influence of the strait-laced, religious, sensible but governess-like Madame de Maintenon, whom he finally married in 1683.

Religious Affairs

The first fruits of his hardening of the arteries showed themselves in religious matters. Till now Louis had been a sore trial, both to his own confessors and to the Pope. As a man he had set an example of loose living—dignified, splendid, but undeniable loose living; and as a king he had asserted the liberties of France vis-à-vis the Pope in no uncertain terms. At the outset of his reign he had forced the Pope to apologize for an attack on the French Ambassador to the Vatican by the Corsican Papal Guard—although the attack had been provoked by the insufferable behaviour of the Ambassador, the Duc de Créqui. Since then there had been a running quarrel over the right of appointment to bishoprics in France and the right to the revenues of vacant sees. Louis had certainly not been a model churchman.

Repression of Huguenots

But that did not prevent him from insisting on obedience to himself from the Church in France; and in his middle age he began to demand more than simple discipline; he wanted uniformity. In spite of the loyalty of the Huguenots to the Crown during the Fronde years, and their valuable contributions to the economy of France by which Colbert set so much store, Louis came to feel that the existence of Protestants within his realm was a disgrace.

The Dragonnades

He tackled the problem in his usual two ways: by bribery followed by force. He set up a fund called the "Treasury of Conversion", and bribed perhaps 50,000 Huguenots to declare themselves converted to Catholicism. Then, in 1681, he excluded Protestants from all Government posts and from all liberal professions. Irritated by these measures and by the missions to convert them, some Huguenots rose in revolt. The rising was ruthlessly put down, and after it Louis quartered dragoons in the houses of the Protestants, with free licence to behave as badly as they liked, until the Huguenots should declare themselves converted in order to get rid of them.

The Revocation of the Edict of Nantes, 1685

A great many conversions followed, though probably most were made with mental reservations. At any rate the success of his brutal policy seemed great enough for Louis to believe what his advisors told him, that the number of Huguenots left in the kingdom was now negligible. At last he felt in a position to take the final step: and in 1685 he formally revoked the Edict of Nantes. All Protestant churches were to be demolished; all their ministers were to leave France within a fortnight or be sent to the galleys.

At once the best of the Huguenots began to leave the country.

They were forbidden to do so, but they went just the same, though the penalty was at first the galleys, and two years later death, for those caught trying to emigrate. In ones and twos, families and convoys, they slipped over the frontiers, till in the end probably 300,000 had gone. They could take little property with them; but they took their energy, their brains, and their knowledge of the industrial processes in which France had just begun to lead Europe. And they took also a hatred of the king who had treated them so brutally, so that their presence in Switzerland, Germany, Holland and England became a perpetual warning to those who met them of the dangers threatened by Louis' despotism. The Revocation of the Edict of Nantes not only helped to postpone the Industrial Revolution in France for perhaps a hundred years: it also helped on the development of the Protestant states, and it led directly to the formation of a coalition against Louis, the League of Augsburg, formed in 1686.

Jansenism

Before leaving religious questions we must look at the other quarrel which disturbed the peace of the Church. And if it seems all a little absurd and remote to us now, we must remember that in seventeenth-century France religious affairs excited almost as much interest as politics, and that even at the beginning of the eighteenth century an English traveller noted that "whereas in Italy civility forbids you to ask strangers their religion, in France you have hardly exchanged three words with your neighbour before he asks you to what confession you belong."

Mère Angélique

In 1599 an eight-year-old girl had become coadjutrix to the convent of Port-Royal des Champs, about twenty miles south-west of Paris. She was Jacqueline Arnauld, in religion

Versailles, 1664

Versailles, 1722

Mother Angélique. At eleven she became Abbess, and at seventeen she undertook to reform the Convent, where the rule had become slack. She then came under the influence of the Abbé de St. Cyran, a fervent admirer of Cornelius Jansen, Bishop of Ypres, whose life of St. Augustine was published in 1640, two years after his death.

The Five Propositions

This work emphasized the teachings of St. Augustine in favour of predestination and personal purity of life. Its views were welcomed by all those Catholics with what may be called Puritan instincts; and were at once seen to be hostile to the teachings of the Jesuits, who believed in man's free will and in working in and through the world, rather than in trying to cut oneself off from the world in order to remain unspotted by it. In 1653 the Pope published a Bill condemning as heretical five propositions, said to be found in Jansen's book.

Port-Royal des Champs

Meanwhile Mère Angélique and her nuns had left Port-Royal des Champs for Paris in 1625, only to return to it in 1648 when their Paris quarters grew too cramped. In the interval a number of pious gentlemen had occupied the convent and founded a school there; and when the nuns returned, these "Solitaires" moved out to a farm and some houses on the opposite slope of the valley, and continued their life of meditation and teaching. They were soon joined by Blaise Pascal, one of the most brilliant mathematicians, philosophers and prose writers of the century: and, as we have seen, one of their pupils was Jean Racine, whose knowledge of Greek tragedy was taught to him by the Jansenist M. Lancelot.

This simple, devout community defended itself as best it could against the Jesuits and the Pope: and in particular Pascal's superb *Lettres Provinciales* won much support for them. But

L

Louis was surrounded by Jesuits, and, what was perhaps more important, he was offended by the connection of Port-Royal with many of the leaders of the Frondes. So in 1660 he had the *Lettres Provinciales* burned by the common hangman. The nuns and their spiritual advisers continued to argue that the Five Propositions, though indeed heretical, were not in fact to be found in Jansen's book: and when Louis asked the Pope to name a Commission to judge these ladies ("pures comme des anges mais fières comme des démons", as the Archbishop of Paris described them) he suddenly found half his clergy arrayed on their side, because they claimed that this Commission was an unwarrantable Papal interference with the affairs of the Gallican Church.

The End of Port-Royal

Louis, only too eager to assert the liberties of the Church of France, thought it over and decided to make peace; which he did in 1668 (with the incidental result that he felt strong enough to defy the Archbishop of Paris and permit the performance of Molière's *Tartuffe* at last in 1669). For a time all seemed calm. But when the Jansenists continued to criticize the Jesuit morality, persecution began again. In 1679 the convent of Port-Royal was forbidden to accept any more novices. And after a fresh quarrel and a fresh Papal Bull in 1706, the twenty-five nuns still alive in it were first forbidden to receive the sacraments, and then, in 1709, were turned out of their house by 300 soldiers commanded by a lieutenant-general of police. The building was razed to the ground, which was ploughed up and salted, and even the bones of those buried there were dug up, and either given to their families or heaped up in a communal grave.

The Bull Unigenitus, 1713

It was a savage and overbearing gesture, typical of Louis in his old age. But it did not solve the controversy, which (as Stendhal showed in *Le Rouge et le Noir*) was still alive in a modified form a hundred years later. Louis' final act was to get the Pope, in the Bull Unigenitus in 1713, to condemn 101 propositions of the Jansenist Père Quesnel ("Why the odd one?" asked the wags, "were 100 not enough?"). But Gallican-Jansenism was still very much alive, and on Louis' death the Regent at once appointed de Noailles, the Archbishop of Paris who had done his best to protect Port-Royal in its last years, to the post of President of the *Conseil de Conscience*.

Foreign Affairs

The Réunions

The next side of Louis' rule that we must look at is his land-grabbing, with the wars that it brought on. No sooner was the Dutch War over than he appointed in 1679 the *Chambre des Réunions*, composed of members of the *Parlements* of Metz, Breisach and Besançon, to look up old treaties and charters and lay claim in Louis' name to any town or district which had ever admitted French overlordship. Now there were, in the no-man's-land between old France and the Empire, many such regions which at one time or another had played off one powerful neighbour against another, and in doing so had put themselves under French protection for a while. In the next six years or so, without firing a shot, Louis thus acquired for France the Saar district, those parts of Alsace not given her by the Treaty of Westphalia, and a great deal of Lorraine.

The League of Augsburg

He backed up this peaceful aggression by strengthening his army and navy, and set Vauban to fortify all his frontier towns. As a result of this and of the Revocation of the Edict of Nantes in 1685, the League of Augsburg was formed against him by the Emperor, Spain, Sweden and the major German princes. Louis' attitude was symbolized by the statue he had put in the Place des Victoires. It represented Louis trampling on Cerberus (symbol of the Triple Alliance) while two allegorical figures standing for the Elbe and the Oder paid homage to him, and the King of Sweden was personified as a slave in chains.

All Europe was against him except Holland, Savoy and England: and he proceeded to add them to his enemies by a typical miscalculation. James II would not agree to help him either actively or passively, and in fact made England useless as an ally by trying to revive the fortunes of the English Catholics. Louis decided to teach him a lesson by doing nothing to stop William of Orange from sailing over to displace him. Unfortunately for Louis, William was instantly successful, and as he was Louis' most implacable enemy, Holland and England joined the enemy camp.

War—1688–97

Louis had already started the war by forcibly installing his own candidate as Archbishop of Cologne, and by invading the Palatinate in support of the claims of Madame, his sister-in-law, whose brother the Elector Palatine had died in 1685. This war now dragged horribly on for nine years, until a sort of stalemate was reached. Louis' main aims were to keep what he had gained in the north-east, and to restore James to the English throne. Fighting went on on five fronts—the Pyrenees, Savoy, the Rhineland, the Netherlands and Ireland.

The Second Devastation of the Palatinate

The Rhineland was effectively neutralized after 1689 by the brutal and systematic devastation of the Palatinate. When Louis' general Montclar complained that at Mannheim he could not get the inhabitants to destroy their own houses, but had to make his troops do it themselves, and that even then the

Germans insisted on living in the ruins, Louis' reply was to order that any found doing so should be killed.

At sea France was successful for a time, until the Battle of La Hogue (1692) destroyed the main French fleet. By that time all James's followers had been mopped up in England and Ireland, and as Louis was finding it increasingly difficult to raise money, he concentrated what he had on the army and starved the Fleet. But on land there was only marching and counter-marching and a series of indecisive engagements, the French still having a superior general in Luxembourg until his death in 1695, while the Allies had superior resources. By 1697 everyone was sick of the struggle, and when the Duke of Savoy had been bribed to desert his allies, the war came to an end. By the Treaty of Ryswick Louis recognized William as King of England, gave back Lorraine to its Duke, and restored to Spain the towns he had taken by reunion or war since 1678; but he kept Strasbourg and the Saarland.

The Spanish Succession

The peace proved only to be a truce, however: in fact, in the last twenty-seven years of Louis' reign the war only stopped for these four years. In 1700 Charles II of Spain died, and it was found in his Will that he had left the crown of Spain to Louis' grandson, Philip of Anjou. There were other claimants to the throne besides the descendants of Louis' wife, Maria-Theresa; and in order to avoid a war Louis had, only a year before, signed the second Partition Treaty, by which the Emperor was to be given Spain, the Netherlands and the Indies, while France took the Spanish lands in Italy. But when the news reached Paris of the Will, made by Charles in the hope of keeping the Spanish dominions together and intact, Louis almost without hesitation accepted the Spanish throne on behalf of his grandson.

Some historians have defended Louis' action on the grounds

that the French claim was the best, and that it would have taken a war anyway to enforce the Partition Treaty. If Louis had refused the offered crown for his grandson, the Spanish envoys were going on to Vienna to offer it to the Emperor—who would then be unlikely to give up Naples, Sicily and the Milanese to France. If Louis had to fight, he might as well fight for the crown itself, with the feeling that right was on his side.

That does not, however, explain his next three actions. He might, just possibly, have avoided a war by announcing that his grandson now renounced all claims to the French throne, to which he was only third in the succession. On the contrary, Louis flatly refused to announce any such thing, and insisted that Philip's right of succession remained unaltered. Next he turned the Dutch garrisons out of the so-called "barrier fortresses" on the northern frontier, and occupied them with French troops; and finally, when James II died, he made the empty but insulting gesture of recognizing the "Old Pretender" as James III, the legitimate King of England. These are the actions of an arrogant, ambitious man, who still thought he could defeat all Europe, and link the Spanish and French Empires in an unassailable union.

War, 1701–14

The war that followed lasted until 1714, and was distinguished by Marlborough's brilliant series of victories over the French in Germany and the Netherlands. In Spain, too, all went well for the Allies for a time, and Philip was twice driven from Madrid. But when all seemed lost Louis refused to make peace; and when French successes in Spain had restored Philip's position there, when Marlborough's influence was nullified by the fall of the Whig Ministry in England in 1710, and when the French victory of Denain in 1712 had decided the Dutch to retire from the long struggle, Louis was able to demand better terms which, harsh though they were, seemed to him acceptable.

Philip kept Spain, but renounced the right of succession in France. He gave up Gibraltar and Minorca to England, with trading rights in South America. Austria took the Netherlands (modern Belgium), Milan, Sardinia and Naples. Sicily went to Savoy. France had to accept the Hanoverian succession in England, and to cede to her Newfoundland and Nova Scotia, Hudson Bay and St. Kitts.

Thus the twenty-three years of war at the end of Louis' reign had brought France only Strasbourg, the Saar, and part of Luxembourg, and a barren family alliance with Spain; while they had cost her a large slice of her colonial empire and the exhaustion of her Treasury, not to mention a series of peasants' revolts and the hatred of half Europe. Even Louis must have felt some of the shame and bitterness of it, though he was not the man to admit that it was caused by his own pride and greed.

Louis as an Old Man

For in spite of the defeats and the growing weakness of France, the chorus of praise had never stopped around the "Roi Soleil", and he had grown so used to adulation that he could not do without it. Saint-Simon records that in his later years Louis liked people to stammer, become confused and seem completely overawed when they spoke to him. It was the period of extravagant compliments like that of Polignac, who praised Marly so much that when caught in a shower there, he said: "A Marly la pluie ne mouille pas."

Flattery

When Louis stayed with the Duc d'Antin he admired the house, but suggested that the landscape was marred by a certain avenue of trees. When he got up next morning they were gone: d'Antin had had them all cut down in the night, and an army of workmen had removed them and turfed over the place where they had stood. And one day Louis sent a footman with a message to Montbazon, Governor of Paris. Montbazon took his hat off to the man, remained uncovered as if in the King's presence, and kept him to dinner. Louis, when told, applauded the gesture and said it was truly gentlemanly behaviour.

Surrounded for fifty years by courtiers like these, it is hardly surprising that Louis ended by feeling that he could do no wrong; and the conviction would be strengthened by his consciousness that he never shirked what he felt to be his duty, that he worked long hours with his Ministers and played his kingly part throughout. He was a mixture of strong appetites and great self-control, a perfect recipe for an autocrat.

His appetite

It was in these later years, in fact, that his fabulous appetite for food began to be noticed. He never touched food between meals, but as he said himself, once he had tasted the first spoonful of soup he could not stop until he was satisfied—and it took plenty to satisfy him. "J'ai souvent vu le Roi" (writes Madame) "manger quatre pleines assiettes de soupes diverses, un faisan entier, une perdrix, une grande assiette de salade, deux grandes tranches de jambon, du mouton au jus ou à l'ail, une assiette de pâtisserie, et puis encore du fruit et des œufs durs." In his room at night, in case he felt hungry after all that, there were always three loaves, two bottles of wine, some water and three cold dishes; and in 1708 when he was ill he ate for supper four wings of chicken, a leg, the breasts of three chickens and a *potage*, which would be a solid dish of boiled meat or fish.

But the truth was that he was a sick man. Gifted by nature with a splendid constitution, "fait pour vivre cent ans", he was now beginning to feel the effects of the attentions of his doctors. One may laugh at Molière's picture of the doctors of the day, but one can only shudder at the reading of the *Journal de la santé du Roi*, kept by the last three of the four doctors who prescribed for him during his reign, Vautier, Vallot, Daquin and Fagon.

They bled him and purged him until one wonders how he could possibly carry out his royal duties. He was never allowed to leave for a campaign, or even travel to Fontainebleau, without having been thoroughly purged first; and the purges, which contained such ingredients as powdered viper, powdered crayfish, tannin, and horse-dung, were so violent that one of them might cause him as many as seventeen visits to the *chaise percée*. They caused internal bleeding, and finally chronic gastro-enteritis, but the doctors continued to treat him for everything except the real evil—incidentally differing in their diagnoses, since Daquin said Louis was bilious, while Fagon said he was lymphatic.

Louis might sometimes rebel, but he could not escape entirely. "N'ayant pu persuader à Sa Majesté de se laisser purger, j'ai dû me contenter avec la saignée, et puis la laisser en repos quelque temps", writes Vallot one day. Within an hour of an operation for a fistula in 1686, he was bled from the arm; and operations in those days, without anaesthetics, were torture. No wonder that Louis felt the need for food. And yet the food he ate was providing him with little or no nourishment, because his surgeons had made such a mess of his mouth that he could not masticate it.

In 1686 they had decided to remove all his upper teeth on the left side: and they were so clumsy that they took away as well a large part of the jaw-bone, so that the rest became decayed and the palate was perforated. The pain caused may be judged from the horrible observation by the Royal doctor that food and drink occasionally passed through the hole in the palate and came out through his nose. He soon lost all his other teeth as well; and so the vast quantities of food which he consumed merely added to the irritation of his intestines without nourishing him, and were largely evacuated undigested, as his doctors also noted.

Court life

All this forces one to admire Louis' heroic courage and endurance; but it also explains why he seemed to become ever more spoiled and autocratic, making life at Court ever more rigid and dull.

Even Louis felt the strain, and liked more to retreat, first to the Trianon, and when that developed its own etiquette, to Marly. Here he did relax a little; but not completely, as poor Mme de Torcy, the wife of the Minister for Foreign Affairs, found. She came in one day, and finding no one at table except the Princesses, she humbly took a seat near the bottom. The Princesses kindly beckoned her up. Protesting, she finally moved next to them, and when the Duchesse de Duras came in she offered to move down, but the Duchess would not let her. But when Louis came in and saw it he was furious. He fixed her with an angry eye, threw her into the utmost confusion, and finally stamped from the room, saying later to Madame de Maintenon that he had never seen such impudence in his life, and that it had completely taken away his appetite.

When his grandson, the Duc de Bourgogne, married the gay and charming Princess of Savoy, life at Court brightened considerably for a time. It has already been mentioned, however, how little he cared for her health, compared with his own pleasure in her company and his insistence on Court rules being observed. And then came the wars and the consequent shortness of money. The splendid gold and silver furnishings of Versailles had to be sold and melted down and replaced by wood and stone. Louis found himself once reduced to showing Samuel Bernard, a Jewish money-lender, round the gardens of Marly, in order to flatter him into lending money to the exhausted Treasury.

Loss of his Family

Finally came domestic tragedy. In 1705 the Duc de Bretagne, his first great-grandson, died at the age of one. In 1711 the Dauphin, his son, died of smallpox. In 1712, within three weeks, he lost the Duc and Duchesse de Bourgogne, and their eldest surviving son, the second Duc de Bretagne. In 1714 his last grandson but one, the Duc de Berry, died. All that was left of his family was the King of Spain and an ailing great-grandson, the future Louis XV, who had in fact been saved because he was not so important as the direct heirs, and so had been left to the care of a sensible nurse when he was ill, and escaped the attentions of the doctors.

After the death of the Bourgognes Louis did say to Villars, to whom he was giving command of his last army as the Allies prepared to march on Paris: "Dieu me punit, je l'ai bien mérité; j'en souffrirai moins dans l'autre monde." And there is gallantry in the rest of his message, in which he rejected the advice of his courtiers to withdraw with the Government to Blois, saying that he felt sure he could hold the line of the Somme. If it had not worked, we might call it stubborn stupidity. But it succeeded, Villars defeated the Allies at Denain, and Louis was able to save a remnant of honour from defeat.

Louis XIV was a terrifying illustration of the saying that the road to Hell is paved with good intentions. For the good of their souls, as he saw it, he had persecuted and exiled half a million Huguenots. For the good of his country, as he saw it, he had plunged her into war after war and almost fatally weakened her. For the good of the monarchy, as he understood it, he had cut both King and Court off from the people, and isolated the monarch behind a living zareba of courtiers at Versailles. He tried to do his Royal duty by working hard, but had thereby made it impossible to find any Ministers who were not mediocrities.

THE BOURBONS

Descended from St. Louis through the Dukes of Vendôme.

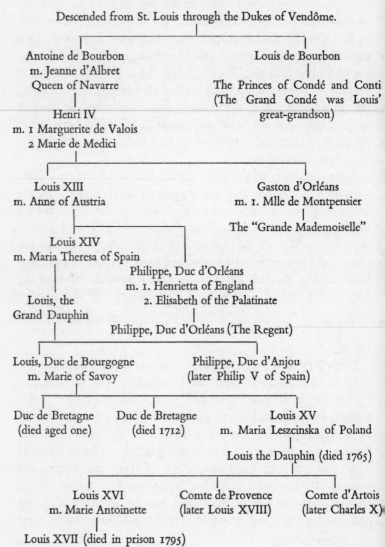

Antoine de Bourbon
m. Jeanne d'Albret
Queen of Navarre

Louis de Bourbon

The Princes of Condé and Conti
(The Grand Condé was Louis'
great-grandson)

Henri IV
m. 1 Marguerite de Valois
2 Marie de Medici

Louis XIII
m. Anne of Austria

Gaston d'Orléans
m. 1. Mlle de Montpensier

The "Grande Mademoiselle"

Louis XIV
m. Maria Theresa of Spain

Philippe, Duc d'Orléans
m. 1. Henrietta of England
2. Elisabeth of the Palatinate

Louis, the
Grand Dauphin

Philippe, Duc d'Orléans (The Regent)

Louis, Duc de Bourgogne
m. Marie of Savoy

Philippe, Duc d'Anjou
(later Philip V of Spain)

Duc de Bretagne
(died aged one)

Duc de Bretagne
(died 1712)

Louis XV
m. Maria Leszcinska of Poland

Louis the Dauphin (died 1765)

Louis XVI
m. Marie Antoinette

Comte de Provence
(later Louis XVIII)

Comte d'Artois
(later Charles X)

Louis XVII (died in prison 1795)

His tragedy was that he lived too long. If he had died in 1679, peaceful development in France would still have been possible. But he lived for another thirty-six years, and by the end he had so firmly riveted on France the ideas and methods of the 1650's that she could only unshackle herself by a revolution.

CHAPTER FOURTEEN

THE STATE OF FRANCE

LOUIS XIV was really the first of the benevolent despots. Taught by Mazarin, he was modelled on the Prince of Machiavelli, of whom Mazarin's friend Naudé said: "Tout le monde blâme cet auteur, et tout le monde le suit, et principalement ceux qui le blâment." The Prince wished to see his State powerful and well governed, and Louis intended France to be both.

The Intendants

His idea of good government was strong government, stemming directly from himself. So by the end of his reign the whole of France was closely controlled by the *intendants*, direct agents of the royal authority, and all rival authorities in the provinces had been suppressed or superseded. Many of the Provincial Estates had ceased to meet—those of Normandy, Berry, Anjou and Touraine among them—and those which still met had been weakened by filling them with Government nominees, and had been bribed and bullied into becoming mere rubber stamps for decisions taken in Versailles. They voted the taxes they were told to vote; in return their members were let off a few taxes themselves, and they had completely ceased to represent or defend the interests of their provinces.

The End of Provincial Liberties

The provincial governors still existed, but they were mere figureheads. They were still very highly paid and received every possible honour, but they could not move a militiaman

or raise a *sou* in taxes without the permission of the *intendant*. In
the towns, the municipal councils were no longer elected but
chosen by the central authorities—and as the councils had
always made a good deal of money out of cheating the rate-
payers, the ordinary citizen did not complain at the change. He
and Louis would both have agreed with Pope that "Whate'er
is best administered is best": and no voice was raised in protest
when finally, in 1692, even the mayor ceased to be elected, and
his office was sold to the highest bidder.

The *intendants* were men of middle-class origin, frequently
of legal training. They were never sent into their own native
provinces to work, and were often chosen by Louis from
among such bodies as the eighty-odd *rapporteurs* to the *Conseil
Privé*, the King's supreme court of appeal. No one could buy
the post of *intendant*, but he could put himself in line for it by
buying a place as *rapporteur* or *maître des requêtes*, and these
places therefore fetched high sums when one was going for
sale. There is not much evidence that the *intendants* grew
inordinately rich, though no doubt they did well out of their
posts; but the great attraction was the power which they
wielded. They were responsible for supervising the administration of justice and the collection of the taxes, for control of
industry and commerce and public education (primary education became compulsory in 1698), for control of the police
(such as it was), of the troops in the area, and of the municipal
and parish finances. Even the village *curé* was almost as much
the servant of the *intendant* as of the bishop, collecting statistical
data for him, reading out the news and Government
proclamations from the pulpit and, as we have seen, announcing
gloomily each year how much the village had to raise in taxes.

The Nobles

There were no rivals to the *intendants*. In spite of the fact that
only one plot to revolt was made by a nobleman in the whole

reign (de Rohan's stupid and abortive plot to hand over Quillebœuf to Holland in 1674, which cost him his head), Louis nevertheless never trusted his nobility. The only great nobleman who ever became a Minister under him was the Duc de Beauvilliers. The others were kept dancing under his watchful eye at Versailles, where they were reduced to complete dependence by the ruinous strain of the style of living demanded of them.

The Expense of Noble Living

According to Mme de Maintenon, who had known poverty and would have sensible ideas, a noble family living at Court as simply as possible in 1680 would need three maids, four footmen, two valets, and two coachmen; and the annual cost of such a household could be 12,000 *livres*—perhaps more than £12,000 to-day—not counting the upkeep of their carriages. A less modest authority, the sieur Audiger, writing in 1692, says that the household of a "person of rank" cannot consist of less than seventy-five servants, and that he must keep twenty-one carriage-horses and twenty riding-horses in his stables. In 1675 a mere *conseiller* (a Q.C. or Under-Secretary) kept a secretary, a squire, two valets, a concierge, a *maître d'hôtel*, a head pantry-man, a kitchen maid, two pages, six footmen, two coachmen, two postillions, and six stablemen; and his wife had a personal maid, two other maids and six housemaids.

In a great household, such as that of M. de Pontchartrain, there were 113 servants; in the Hôtel de Nevers 146. And none of these servants were ever dismissed when they grew too old to work: they were pensioned or given light work, while their children had to be given dowries and a start in life. No wonder that the old *noblesse d'épée* began in the country to sink to the level of gentleman-farmers, or in Court circles to depend more and more on marriage to the daughters of wealthy commoners, or on the King's bounty.

Decline of the smaller Nobility

In 1707 Vauban wrote in his *Dîme Royale*:

> La vie errante que je mène depuis quarante ans et plus m'ayant donné occasion de voir et visiter plusieurs fois, et de plusieurs façons, la plus grande partie des provinces de ce royaume, tantôt seul avec mes domestiques, tantôt en compagnie de quelques ingénieurs, j'ai souvent eu occasion de donner carrière à mes réflexions et de remarquer le bon et le mauvais état des pays; d'en examiner l'état et la situation, et celui des peuples, dont la pauvreté ayant souvent excité ma compassion m'a donné lieu d'en rechercher la cause. Les grands chemins de la campagne et les rues des villes et des bourgs sont pleins de mendiants, que la faim et la nudité chassent de chez eux. Par toutes les recherches que j'ai pu faire depuis plusieurs années que je m'y applique, j'ai fort bien remarqué que dans ces derniers temps près de la dixième partie du peuple est réduite à la mendicité et mendie effectivement; que des neuf autres parties il y en a cinq qui ne sont pas en état de faire l'aumône à celle-là; des quatre autres parties qui restent les trois sont fort malaisées, et embarrassées de dettes et de procès; et que dans la dixième où je mets tous les gens d'épée, de robe, ecclésiastiques et laïques, toute la noblesse haute, la noblesse distinguée et les gens en charges militaires et civiles, les bons marchands, les bourgeois rentés et les plus accommodés, on ne peut pas compter sur cent mille familles, et je ne crois pas mentir quand je dirai qu'il n'y en a pas dix mille qu'on puisse dire être fort à leur aise; et qui en ôterait les gens d'affaires, leurs alliés et adhérents couverts, et ceux que le Roi soutient par ses bienfaits, quelques marchands, etc., je m'assure que le reste serait en petit nombre.

"Ceux que le Roi soutient par ses bienfaits . . ."—they were all right. So were "les gens en charges militaires et civiles . . ." But the smaller nobility, who could not afford Versailles life or still felt tied to their lands, sank lower and lower, till they became merely the largest landowners in the village, the butt of satirists like Molière with his M. de Pourceaugnac and his Comtesse d'Escarbagnas, and the prey of the financiers who were rising as the gentry sank.

Finance

For the finances of the State were in the same old muddle as

M

before, or worse. Colbert had seen that they needed reform, but he had not dared attempt the radical changes that were essential. Like Sully, he had merely tidied up here and there. In some ways, in fact, he had made life more burdensome by his attempts to control the whole economic life of France. He had formed great overseas trading companies, which had all failed or drifted into semi-stagnation, while at the same time keeping their monopolies so that the enterprising private trader had no chance. He had interfered in the minutest details, as when he laid down that the innkeepers of Chevreuse were only to sell food and drink to the ribbon-makers of the town for one hour a day, because he thought that the ribbon industry was not prospering through the idleness of the workers in it. He would send out to the colony in Canada a convoy of "150 girls, with horses, stallions and ewes", and then order that the soldiers there must marry the girls within a fortnight of the convoy's arrival, and would be fined if they had no children before the year was up.

The Failure of Colbert's attempts at Reform

Though well-intentioned, this was despotism, and as soon as things began to go wrong, they went very wrong. Colbert's own protectionist system helped to bring on the first major war, the Dutch War of 1670; that and the succeeding wars defeated all attempts to reform the financial and administrative system. Colbert had thought at first of abolishing the caste system in the holding of offices, and in the years 1660–70 the prices of judicial and administrative offices were successively reduced, with the aim of making possible their purchase by the State and a new system of appointment. But by 1678 it was clear that the State could not even afford to buy them in at a reduced price: so not only were the prices raised again, but more and more offices were put up for sale, until by 1700 even the municipal elections were abolished and the office of mayor in towns and villages was added to all the others which could be bought.

The "Capitation"

Similarly, Colbert had reduced the *aides* and internal *douanes* as a first step towards a saner financial system; but by 1701, eighteen years after his death, not only had they risen again, but a new tax, the *capitation*, had been added on top of all the others to pay for the wars. By this, every Frenchman was placed in one of twenty-two classes according to rank and wealth, and had to pay from 2000 *livres* a year in the top class down to one *livre* in the lowest class. Of course, the privileged classes managed to get their assessments reduced as usual, the clergy made a down payment as a body at a low rate per head, many provinces succeeded in getting similar *abonnements* accepted, and it was only the middle classes and the country nobles who had to pay the full tax.

Nor was this the last addition. In 1710 came the *dixième*, a tax of a tenth on income from lands, dividends or salaries. Everyone behaved as before, and the middle and lower classes shouldered yet another burden. They had already seen their money depreciating in value, since it was a time of inflation, and Louis' Ministers, even including Colbert, had not hesitated to debase the coinage on occasion. Many of them had been hit by Colbert's first move after ousting Fouquet, when he declared the State bankrupt and cancelled a large part of the public debt. It was no wonder that the Frenchman already distrusted banks and Government finance, and was an inveterate hoarder of gold in a 'stocking in the chimney.'

Yet all this was not enough to pay for the wars. At Colbert's death the budget deficit was already 16 million *livres*: by 1697 the expenses were 219 million and the regular receipts only 81 million. The extra 138 million had to be found by the sale of offices, lotteries, State bankruptcy again, and loans from wealthy financiers. The revenues for years to come were mortgaged, just as they had been by poor Fouquet; and it is worth noting in passing that not even Fouquet, not even perhaps Mazarin, had amassed such an enormous personal fortune as the 'honest' man who got Fouquet condemned to perpetual imprisonment, Colbert himself.

The Rise of the "Noblesse de Robe"

As in the days of Fouquet, the big financiers, money-lenders, and the farmers of the taxes were growing fabulously rich. So, too, were the officials of justice and the administration, who were taking the place of the country nobles in the national hierarchy. Some of them must have been very rich, since the office of *Président à Mortier du Parlement de Paris* sold for 500,000 *livres* in 1684, and the same office at Rouen for 150,000 *livres*. A *conseiller's* office cost 100,000 at Paris, 42,000 at Dijon, and so on. And yet these offices did not bring in much direct return in cash to their holders. They were either indirectly valuable, or paid for with the profits of previous jobs, or else bought by a financier as a present for an official from whom he expected, or had already received, useful favours. They did carry immense social prestige, too. In the provinces the First President of the *Parlement* entered a city to the sound of cannon when the *Parlement* met; he passed under triumphal arches bearing his coat of arms, and took precedence over all but the highest nobility.

These officials bought their offices for life, and could not be dismissed by the Government. They were therefore ready to act independently on occasion, and were in fact the only obstacle to Louis' despotism. They had no influence on the formation of policy or on the King's decisions; but they could refuse to carry them out. For instance, judges were urged to condemn criminals to the galleys, which were always short of men. In 1662 the *intendant* of Poitou announced to the Minister that he had twenty good, strong prisoners for the galleys, adding: "Quand il vous plaira, vous ferez partir un commissaire pour les prendre, et le plus tôt sera le meilleur, afin qu'ils ne dépérissent pas." But a few weeks later he writes to say he has only been able to send five after all, explaining: "On n'est pas bien maître des juges." There were many such cases, where orders from the centre were simply not carried out by the provincial officials. Louis broke the corporate power of the *Parlements*, but he could not tame all their individual members.

The Common People

The state of all these upper and middle classes can be estimated fairly easily from official correspondence and records. What is much harder to gauge is the condition of the workers and peasants. Early in the century no one had bothered about them, and Richelieu could write harshly: "Tous les politiques sont d'accord que, si les peuples étaient trop à leur aise, il serait impossible de les contenir dans leur devoir." By the end of the century a more sensitive spirit was abroad. Mme de Sévigné tells the story of how the Archbishop of Rheims drove to Paris:

> L'archevêque de Reims revenait hier fort vite de Saint-Germain, c'était comme un tourbillon: il croit bien être grand seigneur; mais ses gens le croient encore plus que lui. Ils passaient au travers de Nanterre, tra, tra, tra; ils rencontrent un homme à cheval, gare, gare: ce pauvre homme veut se ranger; son cheval ne veut pas: et enfin le carrosse et les six chevaux renversent le pauvre homme et le cheval, et passent par dessus, et si bien par dessus que le carrosse en fut versé et renversé: en même temps l'homme et le cheval, au lieu de s'amuser à être roués et estropiés, se relèvent miraculeusement, remontent l'un sur l'autre, et s'enfuient, et courent encore, pendant que les laquais de l'archevêque et le cocher, et l'archevêque même se mettent à crier: "Arrête, arrête ce coquin, qu'on lui donne cent coups." L'archevêque, en racontant ceci, disait: "Si j'avais tenu ce maraud-là, je lui aurais rompu les bras et coupé les oreilles."

Not a nice man, the Archbishop: but Mme de Sévigné herself clearly disapproves. And the end of the century

produced, besides the passage from Vauban quoted above, at
least two other cries of sympathy for the poor peasants, which
have made many people believe that the lot of the humble
Frenchman was wretched indeed. There is the passage of
Fénelon's *Letter to the King* in 1695:

> Yet your people, whom you should love like children, and who have
> till now so passionately loved you, are dying of hunger. The tilling of the
> ground has almost stopped; towns and countryside alike are emptying;
> all trades are so slack that the workers cannot earn a living. All
> commerce has been annihilated. In consequence you have destroyed half
> the real strength of your State, in order to make and defend empty
> conquests abroad. Instead of sucking money from your poor people
> you should give alms to them and feed them. The whole of France is one
> vast hospital, desolate and short of food.

The exaggerations in this are obvious; but one assumes that
it must have a basis of truth, especially since it is backed up by
the famous passage in La Bruyère, too long to quote in its
entirety, but which contains the grim sentence:

> L'on voit certains animaux farouches, des mâles et des femelles, répandus
> par la campagne, noirs, livides et tout brûlés du soleil, attachés à la terre
> qu'ils fouillent et qu'ils remuent avec une opiniâtreté invincible: ils ont
> comme une voix articulée, et quand ils se lèvent sur leurs pieds ils
> montrent une face humaine: et en effet ils sont des hommes.

In 1698 the *intendant* of Berry writes:

> Il n'y a point de nation plus sauvage que ces peuples: on en trouve
> quelquefois des troupes à la campagne, assis en rond au milieu d'une terre
> labourée, et toujours loin des chemins: mais si l'on en approche, cette
> bande se disperse aussitôt.

But it must be noted that both 1695 (when Fénelon wrote)
and 1698 were famine years, with appallingly hard winters
followed by wet summers: and that La Bruyère was a critic of
society, embittered by living as a poor dependant in a great
man's house, and anticipating Jean-Jacques Rousseau with an
attack on the rich, which he ends with the words:

> Ils (*the poor*) épargnent aux autres hommes la peine de semer, de labourer

et de recueillir pour vivre, et méritent ainsi de ne pas manquer de ce pain qu'ils ont semé.

Between the bad years, even during the wars, there must have been periods of reasonable prosperity. How else could the last desperate levies of men in 1710 and 1711 have produced stout enough soldiers to defeat the Allies at Denain? Madame de Sévigné speaks of meeting a tenant's wife in a pretty dress of holland over taffeta which she admires; and her tart comment that she wishes the woman's husband would pay some of the 8,000 *livres* he owes to the estate must surely indicate a considerable farm tenancy. Other travellers speak of finding broad acres of well-kept land even in the poorest regions, presumably the estates of those whose connections could keep their tax assessments low: on such estates the tenants would share their landlord's prosperity.

Only a few years of peace were needed under the Regency to restore France's economy; and the process had already begun whereby, in the century between 1690 and the Revolution, the peasants succeeded in buying for themselves over a quarter of the land of France. That land was rich and fertile, and the climate as a rule was friendly. And from the Frenchman's point of view there was this to be said for Louis' wars: they were mostly fought outside the frontiers of France.

The New Spirit of Criticism

It is nevertheless remarkable that the last two great men of letters in the reign of Louis XIV—La Bruyère and Fénelon—should both have felt bound to say their piece about the miseries of the poor. In spite of Louis' paternalism, which extended to art and letters as much as to everything else, the writers who really belong to his personal reign began to be critical of him. Louis founded the *Académie des Inscriptions et Belles-Lettres* in 1663, that of Painting in 1664, and that of Science in 1666; in 1671 Colbert became a member of the

Académie Française, which in 1672 was given a permanent home in the Louvre. All arts were officially controlled and patronized, and in those days flattery of the King was *de rigueur*. His praise was the set theme in the Academy's competitions for rhetoric and poetry. Molière devoted the last act of *Tartuffe* to flattery of him; Racine wrote: "Tous les mots de la langue, toutes les syllabes nous paraissent précieuses parce que nous les regardons comme autant d'instruments qui doivent servir à la gloire de notre auguste protecteur." But by the end of the century the tone had changed, and even Racine fell out of favour for daring to meddle with politics.

For one thing Louis was not the patron he had been. His 'moral rearmament' of the '80's had turned him against the theatre; his shortage of money in the '90's prevented him from ordering so many new pictures and sculptures. For another thing the ageing and unsuccessful despot was not so inspiring a subject as the handsome and dashing young prince of the early years. For a third, the intellectual climate was changing, however much Louis might pontificate, and insist that nothing should change.

"C'est que le Grand Siècle n'a pas duré autant que le Grand Roi", writes Boulenger. We would take a different view, and say that the greatness of the middle years of the century could not be prolonged under the meddlesome rule of an elderly mediocrity. Looking back from the twentieth century, we may perhaps risk a modern comparison, and remember the words of a Yorkshire coach to the captain of a losing cricket side: "You bowled too long and you bowled too bad." Louis ruled too long; and his idea of how to rule, though honestly held, was narrow and false. Under the glory of his reign there was the rottenness that produced the poisoners; and before his reign was over there had sounded the first rumble of the Revolution, when people in high society had begun to praise the mocking poems of a young Paris wit called Voltaire.

INDEX